Latinos of Boulder County, Colorado, 1900-1980

Volume II:
Lives and Legacies

by

Marjorie K. McIntosh

Distinguished Professor of History Emerita
University of Colorado at Boulder

Written for:
Boulder County Latino History Project

With assistance from:
Longmont Museum

Endorsed by:
**Department of Ethnic Studies,
University of Colorado at Boulder**

 **Old John Publishing**
Palm Springs, California

McIntosh, Marjorie K. (Marjorie Keniston)
The Latinos of Boulder County, Colorado, 1900-1980
Volume II: Lives and Legacies / M.K. McIntosh
180 pages. 229 cm.
Includes bibliographical references.

ISBN 978-0-9863873-4-0 (hardcover)
978-0-9863873-5-7 (paperback)

1. Hispanic Americans–Colorado–Boulder County–History.
2. Colorado–History, Local–20th Century.
3. Boulder County (Colorado)–History.

2015961054

References to Internet Web sites (URLs) were accurate at the time of writing. Neither the author nor Old John Publishing is responsible for URLs that may have expired or changed since the manuscript was prepared.

Contents

Appendices

*Cover: The family of Ed and Delia Vargas Tafoya
in front of their house on Water Street, Boulder in 1956.
Courtesy of Mable Stewart*

Abbreviations and Notes

Abbreviations:

BCLHP   Boulder County Latino History Project

CU-Boulder University of Colorado at Boulder

ICE   Immigration and Customs Enforcement,
            U.S. government

LHS   Longmont Hispanic Study

LM   Longmont Museum

LPL   Lafayette Public Library

MROHP   Maria Rogers Oral History Program,
            Carnegie Branch Library for Local History,
            Boulder Public Library

UMAS   United Mexican American Students,
            University of Colorado

VFW   Veterans of Foreign Wars

Illustration captions:

The captions under the illustrations give only the title of the image. For full references, including credits, see the List of Illustrations at the back of the book.

References in footnotes and Sources:

All footnote references are given in a short form. Full references are provided at the back of the book, under Sources. Section A includes sources dealing specifically with Boulder County Latinas/os. Nearly all of these materials are available online; a URL or other form of access is given for each entry. In the online version of this book, references in section A are hyperlinked directly to the original source. Other kinds of material are listed in section B of Sources.

Introduction

Since the beginning of the twentieth century, people from Spanish-speaking backgrounds have played essential roles in Boulder County, Colorado. The first volume in this set offers a chronological and thematic history of local Latinas/os, tracing the contributions they made to this region between 1900 and 1980.[1] Its introductory chapter lays out some background material that applies to this book as well.[2] It summarizes the intellectual context provided by other historical work, discusses ethnic identity and the terms that have been used over time to describe Latinas/os, and gives a brief overview of relevant nineteenth-century history. The chapter also explains how people are designated in this study and that we use gender-inclusive terms to make clear the centrality of women.

The present volume explores the daily lives of Latinas/os. It looks at their families, homes and neighborhoods, social and cultural interactions, religious patterns, and education across the span from 1900 to 1980. It is not a formal or complete sociological analysis but rather a description based on how local Latinas/os talked and wrote about their own experiences and those of their parents and grandparents. Their narratives are enriched by photos preserved within families. Because most of this evidence was provided by members of the community, local people are themselves the producers of historical knowledge, though the book was written by an academic historian. The book draws attention also to legacies, to the ways in which people from Spanish-speaking backgrounds developed attitudes and traditions that continue

---

[1] McIntosh, *Latinos of Boulder County, Colorado, 1900-1980*, Vol. I, *History and Contributions* [cited hereafter as Vol. I]. The same indexing terms are used in both volumes, to make searching easier.

[2] Vol. I, Ch. 1. That book also includes a Foreword by Prof. Arturo Aldama of the Department of Ethnic Studies, University of Colorado at Boulder, the Author's Preface, and Acknowledgments.

in Boulder County today among many Latinas/os and in some cases the wider community too.

Like the first book, this one focuses on three towns within Boulder County that had very different features. Longmont was almost entirely dependent upon commercial agriculture and food processing, while coal mining provided the economic basis for the smaller community of Lafayette. Boulder, the county seat, was a commercial center and home to the University of Colorado. That diversity helps to makes the present study comparable to other communities in the American Southwest.

Both of these studies rely upon the excellent collection of primary sources gathered by the Boulder County Latino History Project [BCLHP] in 2013-14.[3] The 1,600 items include rich personal materials: 100 oral history interviews, family biographies, videos, and hundreds of family photos. Those sources are supplemented by newspaper articles and quantified information about immigration, Latino students in the local schools, and occupations and employers. Virtually all of the primary materials cited in these two volumes are available online.[4] Because a URL is provided for nearly every reference in the printed format, and references in the online versions of the books are live-linked to their sources, anyone who has access to the Web can view the original evidence, without going to a research library or traveling to archives. The study is therefore a perfect educational tool for K-12 and college teachers, enabling students to see the raw material from which historical work is produced.[5]

This book also introduces the BCLHP's remarkable interactive, computer-based maps, one for each of the three towns in every decade between 1926 and 1975.[6] The maps display the location of households headed by people with Latino surnames, using a different color for students. If a viewer clicks on one of the marked households, a window opens with the names of the adult residents, their street address, and for some, their occupations and employers. These unique maps allow us to

---

[3] For these sources and how they were assembled, see Vol. I, Ch. 1B.

[4] Most are on the BCLHP's website (bocolatinohistory.colorado.edu), while others are on those of museums or libraries.

[5] The BCLHP's website has a special section for educators, containing Primary Source Sets, Lesson Plans, short clips from interviews and films, and other instructional materials: teachbocolatinohistory.colorado.edu.

[6] They can be accessed at bocolatinohistory.colorado.edu, under "Interactive City Maps."

study changes in housing patterns and neighborhoods over time.

Although this set is a local study, it sheds light on broader topics important to historians, sociologists, Chican@/Ethnic Studies specialists, and others who focus on the Southwest. Among them are issues of migration, labor conditions, racism and discrimination, the impact of war and veterans, and civil rights activity. The books also explore four interpretive questions: (1) What were the roles, experiences, and contributions of women? (2) How did people interact within families, looking especially at relations between men and women and between generations? (3) To what extent did Boulder County share patterns with communities that lay closer to the heart of the U.S.-Mexican borderlands or were major cities with large Latino populations; and to what extent was it influenced by a local network that included Denver? (4) How did local Latinas/os define themselves, creating an ethnic identity?

The chapters below begin with examination of the settings in which many aspects of Latinas/os' lives took place: their families, including key stages in the course of life; and their houses and neighborhoods. Chapter 3 discusses food, health, and medicine, while Chapter 4 describes social life, entertainment, and sports. Religious activities are next, followed by the education of Latino children. In these accounts, some voices are heard more frequently than others, because they present common patterns with special clarity. Many of the illustrations are old family snapshots, so their photographic quality is not always high, but they provide important visual information. An epilogue jumps 30 years forward to relate the experiences of ten young Latinas/os who worked as interns with the BCLHP in summer, 2013. As they talk about their own lives, we hear both continuities and contrasts with the lives of Boulder County's Latinas/os prior to 1980, and we gain hope for the future. The book ends by highlighting the legacies left by earlier Latinas/os to people today.

Chapter 1

Families and the Stages of Life

The family was the core of most Latinas/os' emotional and social world, providing warmth, companionship, and practical support. Nearly everyone formed part of an immediate family, and many people were involved with members of their extended family. Men as well as women engaged actively with children, and people commonly had close ties with their grandparents and/or grandchildren. The family was where cooking and eating took place and children were raised; especially in the first half of the twentieth century, it was also a setting for health care, cultural activities, and religious worship.[1] Marriage was an economic partnership too: women's work within the home and sometimes outside of it was an essential counterpart to the income that men brought in.[2] If *la familia* was the institution that held *la gente* [the people] together, it was often the strength of women that held families together. The main transitions within the life course, extending from birth to death, were usually marked by gatherings at home. This chapter focuses on families and life stages, drawing attention to changes over time between 1900 and 1980. Later parts of the book include additional information.

A. Families, Parents, and Grandparents

The foundation of most Latino families was the two parents. Although marriages were usually formed as the result of affection between two young people, and although many couples remained tightly bonded throughout their lives, marriage was not defined merely in emotional or sexual terms. David Toledo said in 1978 that he had always found a

---

[1] As discussed in Chs. 3A-B, 4A-B, and 5B below.
[2] See Vol. I, Chs. 3A and D, 5A, and 6C.

way to earn money for his family, as a miner and through other jobs.[3] But they managed only because his wife was working at home, taking care of the household and children.

While men were normally the main authority figures within their families, especially in public contexts, their wives controlled the inner workings of the household, played a major role in their children's lives, and often exerted considerable influence over their husbands and brothers. Mothers organized domestic work and generally did most of it themselves, while at the same time making sure that their children were being cared for and taught important human and practical skills.[4] If a mother was herself fully occupied with household tasks or was employed outside the home, she could usually arrange for an older daughter, grandmother, or other relative to look after the younger children. Patriarchal assumptions and reliance upon unpaid female work were common features of the lives of most American women prior to the 1960s and 1970s, not just Latinas.

Fathers and grandfathers were often described as doing things with their children (singing, playing musical instruments for dancing, or telling them stories) when they were at home in the evenings and on those days when they did not have to work.[5] Reina Gallegos, whose parents had come from New Mexico, adored her father, Alejandro Jaramillo, despite his strict moral standards, and loved to spend time with him.[6] "I used to dance with my father out in the garden, out in the fields. He would sing and I would dance with him." Mary Martinez and her sisters lived with their grandparents northeast of Longmont. She recalled listening to her grandfather, who described himself as an Aztec Indian, as he talked about the ceremonial rituals his parents used to perform at the top of pyramids in Mexico and as he demonstrated Indian dances to them.[7] Many photos preserved by families show fathers with their children, in both earlier and more recent periods.[8]

A recurring theme in these Latino families was the importance of grandparents and sometimes great-grandparents. In some cases,

---

[3] Toledo, David, interview, c. 1978.

[4] For women's work within the household, see Vol. I, Ch. 3D.

[5] See Ch. 4A-B below.

[6] Gallegos, Reina, interview, c. 1987. For Reina's love of dancing as an adult, see Illus. 4.8 below.

[7] Martinez, Mary, interview, 1988. See also "Aztec dancers."

[8] See. e.g., "Father Wearing Hat with Four Children," "Ray Perez with baby," "Tony Quintana holding baby," and "Tony Quintana with three sons."

Illus. 1.1. *Studio portrait of father holding baby girl with two boys*

Illus. 1.2. *Father smoking pipe with two young children*

Illus. 1.3. *Secundino Herrera with children at baby's birthday*

an older couple actually took in and raised their grandchildren. That pattern was common if one of their daughters died or was unable to bring up her children. When Elvinia ("Bea") Martinez Borrego, later of Longmont, was orphaned at age three, she went to live with her grandmother in Cebolla, New Mexico.[9] The older woman supported herself as a midwife and operator of a dancehall. J. H. Cortez and his wife Sabina, who came to the Longmont area as beet workers and settled in the town sometime around 1915, raised seven of their grandchildren after one of their sons-in-law abandoned his family and their daughter died.[10] Juan and Josephine Martinez had ten children between 1924 and 1946, eight of whom lived; in 1943 they adopted their first-born grandchild.[11] Few references were made in the Boulder County sources to illegitimate children, but such babies were apparently raised usually by grandparents or other relatives.

Grandparental involvement with children continued later in the century. Carmen Ramirez, born in 1960 and raised in El Paso, told a powerful story about her grandparents' role in her life.[12] Her birth mother did not want her children and abandoned them in Florida when Carmen was 3 years old and her brother was 18 months. Carmen's grandmother, Juana Olguin Gandara, "being a strong *Mejicana catolica*, said '*Mi sangre no anda rodando*' [My blood does not go running around] and sent my aunt, *mi tia* Concha, who became my mother, to get us in Florida." Juana also bought a suit for her son, the children's father, and sent him along to help bring the children back. She "wanted to make sure that we were raised by family. That was probably the biggest gift." Carmen lived with her grandparents and her aunt Concha until the older people's death.

Grandparents were important in other ways as well. Heriberto ("Beto") Moreno, the son of a bartender, was born in Ciudad Juarez, Mexico.[13] When he was in his teens, around 1960, he came across the border to El Paso, sponsored by his grandparents, who were already living there. Linda Arroyo-Holmstrom, born in 1956, recalled how

---

[9] "Borrego, Albert and Elvinia ("Bea") Martinez, biography." For other grandparents and great-grandparents, see "Madrigal family of Boulder, biographies" and "Five generations of women."

[10] Cordova, Patsy, interview, c. 1987, "Cortez, Jose Hilario ("J. H.") and Maria Sabina, biography," and "Joseph and Sabina Cortez."

[11] "Martinez, Juan and Josephine; Marcella Diaz, biography."

[12] Ramirez, Carmen, interview, 2013, for this and below.

[13] Moreno, Heriberto ("Beto"), interview, 2013.

Illus. 1.4. *Four children with an old woman*

Illus. 1.5. *Mr. and Mrs. Cortez with granddaughter Mercy Martinez and her children*

Illus. 1.6. *Four generations of the Montour family of Lafayette, 1987*

easy it was to skip across from her own backyard in Boulder to her grandparents' house, which was immediately behind them across the alley.[14] The elder generation formed the emotional and physical heart of Linda's large group of relatives.

> It almost seemed like my extended family was my immediate family, because we would get together every Sunday. It was church and then after that everyone would meet at my grandparents' house, the Arroyos' house, and we'd all eat together. That was just typical, and we of course celebrated every birthday. I had eighteen first cousins in Boulder, and so that was my social life too. I didn't need anything other than my immediate and extended family. We were really close, . . . we were so blessed.

Aunts and uncles too might take in children. Carmen and Romaldo Razo came to the Lafayette area in 1914 from Durango, Mexico.[15] They had five children of their own, but they also adopted two nephews and raised another six nieces and nephews after their parents were killed in a car accident. Tom Abila, born around 1933, lived at first with his grandparents, but when his grandmother became bedridden, he moved in with his aunt Sarah.[16] Doris Ogeda Gonzales's mother was left on her own in the early 1930s with three young children when her husband returned to Mexico to visit his ailing mother but was unable to come back across the border.[17] She first found work bottling beer during Prohibition but later cleaned houses in Boulder. When she came down with tuberculosis, she was placed into the local sanitarium. At that point Doris's uncle, Pete Saragosa, and his wife Nellie took in the children. For the next four years they lived in the Saragosas' large household, which included other relatives too.

Even if they did not raise children entirely, aunts and uncles were often vital members of the extended family unit. Canuto and Gregoria Martinez's adult children who were living in Boulder in the 1940s and 1950 were in regular contact thanks to their sister Lola. One of her nephews later wrote a deeply appreciative account of her role within the family. When Carmen Ramirez was living on the streets in El Paso during high school, it was her aunt Concha who came to find her every week, bringing food and other necessities.[18]

---

[14] Arroyo-Holmstrom, Linda, interview, 2013, for this and below.
[15] Montour, Eleanor, interview, 2013.
[16] Abila, Tom, interview, 1978.
[17] Gonzales, Doris, interview, 2013.
[18] Ramirez, Carmen, interview, 2013.

Lola Martinez

Lola Martinez (1913-1974) was born in Pueblo to Canuto and Gregoria Martinez. She was one of ten children. Her days of hard work in the fields alongside her family gave her special sensitivity to those who need a hand up or an ear to just listen. She worked in the defense industry during WWII on the assembly line constructing aircraft. After the war, she returned to work as a domestic servant for well-off families on the "Hill". She was a very proud person. During a Nixon fundraiser in 1960, a young Nixon supporter wanted to pin a Nixon button on her. The young Nixon supporter must have thought domestic servants were a fixture to be decorated. My Aunt Lola spoke up. "Don't pin that Nixon button on me, "I will vote for Kennedy". She could have been fired but she wasn't.

Aunt Lola was known as the glue that kept the extended Martinez family together in good and bad times. Her home was always open to the extended family; to newlyweds who needed a place to stay for a couple of months until moving on to their own home; to a family who had lost a parent; to a family whose primary bread earner had been hurt in an accident; but best of all, her home was open for birthdays, holidays, for baptisms', for making tamales for New Year's; and when the extended Martinez family needed a place to gather. (Espinosa, Hernandez, Madrigal, Pacheco and, of course, Martinez) Aunt Lola epitomized the values and strength, beauty and caring of the Mexican American extended family.

Illus. 1.7. *Biography and photo of Lola Martinez*

Although extended families whose members lived near each other were able to stay in close contact, physical distance and national borders weakened some ties. For immigrants from other countries, it might be difficult to keep in touch through letters or—later—telephone calls; travelling to one's old home might be impossible without the necessary papers.[19] Even among American-born Latinas/os, maintaining family relationships became harder as more people moved around the country in connection with their work, especially after the late 1960s.

Many Latino families prior to the mid-twentieth century were very large, with more children than is common in the 2010s. Because siblings and other relatives who lived nearby could help take care of younger children, they generally received the love and attention they needed to develop well. Indeed, affection for children was part of Latino culture. People liked having big households filled with youngsters of various

---

[19] Such problems disrupted the cultural borderland that in the early twentieth century spanned the southwestern U.S. and northernmost Mexican states (see Vol. I, Ch. 1B). For the impact of the border in the early twenty-first century, see the Epilogue below.

Archuleta Family, 1951

From top left to right: Clara, 19 yrs; Clofes, mother;
Marylou, 14 yrs; Becky 19 yrs; Juan, father; Frank Jr., 2 yrs;
Juanita, 12 yrs; Cora, 25 yrs; Frank Sr. 25 yrs; Delores
Gabriella, cousin, 13 yrs; Richard Gabriella, cousin, 7 yrs;
Archie Archuleta, 5 yrs; Ramona, 9 yrs

*Illus. 1.8. Archuleta
family in 1951*

ages, as reflected in family photos.[20] Further, during the first part of
the twentieth century, children could contribute to the household's net
income.[21] For field workers, the labor of children and teenagers might be
a necessity, and mines offered employment to older boys.

An early age of marriage for women contributed to big families. Prior
to around 1960, some girls married as young as 14 or 15, and most were
married by the time they reached 20. Methods of birth control were not
yet available, so many people of all ethnicities and races had big families.
Even when birth control became readily accessible, the Catholic Church
did not accept its use. Most women breast-fed their babies, which
decreased ovulation and lessened the chances that they would become
pregnant soon after the birth of the previous child. But if a woman had
a baby every two or three years from her mid-teens to her mid-40s,
that would result in something like 10-15 births. The extended range of
years over which women bore children dissolved sharp lines between
generations: people might easily have aunts and uncles younger than
themselves and nieces and nephews who were older.

Some Latino households became larger by taking in unrelated

---

[20] See also Illus. 4.1 below and "Gonzales family portrait."
[21] See Vol. I, Ch. 3D for child labor.

Illus. 1.9. Parents with baby and five other children

children.[22] Teresa Alvarez, born in Zacatecas, Mexico in 1897, came to Boulder with her parents as a child.[23] When they died, she went to live with a foster family who lived in the beet fields near Fort Collins. Roseann Chavez Ortega's Mexican-born grandparents, who were living in Aguilar around 1920, were unable to have children of their own, so they adopted the illegitimate baby of an Italian family; she later became Roseann's mother.[24] Rudy and Theresa Vigil of Lafayette were foster parents for 34 children over a period of 20 years starting in the late 1960s.[25] Very rarely were children placed in orphanages. The only instance of that practice encountered in this study was provided by Dolores Silva, a long-time resident of Lafayette.[26] She was born at home in Denver in 1929, assisted by a black midwife. When her mother, who had come north from Taos, New Mexico, and her father, a professional baseball player, divorced, their older children were sent to an orphanage, but Dolores was a baby and stayed with her mother and step-father.

[22] For abduction of children, as was common in parts of the Southwest until the early twentieth century, see Vol. I, Ch. 2B.
[23] Alvarez, Teresa, interview, 1976.
[24] Ortega, Roseann Chavez, interview, 1986.
[25] "Vigil, Rudy and Theresa, biography."
[26] Silva, Dolores, interview, 2013.

John S. Chavez with his brothers and sister, this picture was taken in Ft. Collins, CO. in 1919.
Front row: John (baby) Louie (seated) Thelma, Ermalinda (seated) Keith
Back row: Ben, Patrick and Larry Chavez

Ermalinda, was the oldest of the children when this picture was taken she was 24 years old. Louie was 21 years old so there was quite a bit of age difference between our Dad (John) and his oldest siblings.

Illus. 1.10. *Eight Chavez siblings in 1919, ranging from a baby to 24 years old*

From the 1960s onwards, family size began to drop, especially among urban residents and people who had gone to high school. In a characteristic sequence, Esther Blazón, the daughter of a field worker, was born in 1943, near the middle of her fifteen brothers and sisters, fourteen of whom survived.[27] Esther's husband William ("Hank") was one of eight children raised on a farm northeast of Longmont. But she and Hank had only three children. Migrant workers and more recent immigrants were likely to have large families right through the twentieth century.

The involvement of men with their children or grandchildren as seen in the Boulder County evidence highlights a contrast between how Latinas/os have traditionally used the term *macho* and the meaning it has acquired in wider American culture. In earlier Latino usage, a man described as *macho* was a good provider for his family in economic terms and a good husband and father, someone who loved his children and enjoyed spending time with them; within the community, he acted with dignity and hoped to win respect from others. The concept of *macho* as referring to a tough young male with attitude and a swagger

[27] Blazón, Esther, interview, 2013.

comes largely from the world of mass media and entertainment, not from within Latino culture itself.

Yet *machismo* had a darker side. The culturally-defined dominance of men within Latino households could potentially serve as a justification for excessive male control over women and children, drinking that squandered the family's resources, and abuse within the home, particularly if a man felt that his authority was being challenged. Although interviews and written accounts of Boulder County's Latinas/os rarely mention problems within marriages, this silence presumably results in part from people's unwillingness to air family difficulties in public. Private conversations indicate that some husbands drank heavily and at times became verbally or physically abusive. Women might be angry with their husbands because of their insistence upon making decisions for the entire family, and at least an occasional wife was not fully committed to her children. Such problems were and still are common within households of all cultural backgrounds, especially those that are living in poverty, where husbands and wives are exhausted from demanding physical labor, and which share cramped and ill-equipped housing.

Even if spouses argued and sometimes fought, however, they rarely divorced. An unhappy couple's relatives would have put great pressure on them to stay together, and the Catholic Church opposed divorce strongly, prohibiting a divorced person from remarrying in a religious ceremony. Further, there were so few good employment opportunities for women outside the family until the later 1960s and 1970s that a woman who left her husband would have found it extremely difficult to support herself and her children, unless her own relatives took them in. So long as a marriage remained an economic partnership and an adequate place for bringing up children, it could continue even if the spouses gained much of their emotional support from their *comadres, compadres*, or other people.

B. Key Stages, Birth to Death

Families formed the setting for the major transition points within the life course of individual people. Until at least the 1960s, mothers generally gave birth to their babies at home, with help only from a midwife or a female relative or friend. Few people mentioned specifically that their mothers or grandmothers had died in childbirth, but the frequency with which older people took in orphaned relatives probably stems in part from that situation.[28] Dora Bernal, who was born in 1911 to a family in the San Luis Valley, was one of four girls and four boys.[29] All the babies were born at home with a midwife assisting except the last, for whose birth a doctor was summoned. Roseann Chavez Ortega, who was living with her parents in a tenant farmer's house east of Boulder in the 1950s, described going with her mother and grandmother to a little shack near them where a Latino beet harvester's family was staying.[30] Her grandmother knew that the family was very poor and that the mother, who had several small children, was pregnant. When they arrived, they found that the woman was already in labor, so Roseann's grandmother delivered the baby and took care of the mother. The baby was born dead or died shortly after birth, whereupon Roseann's grandmother placed the body into a little box and buried it. By the later 1940s, some women—especially those living in towns—gave birth in hospitals. Roy Maestas's mother had been aided by a midwife when he was born in New Mexico in 1909, but his wife's children were born in hospitals in Boulder County.[31]

Families who lived near a church and could afford the payment generally wanted to have their children baptized or christened. This ceremony included giving the baby its formal name and appointing its *padrinos* (godparents).[32] Babies were commonly named after relatives or close friends of their parents. Candace Arroyo said that she had been named after her grandfathers.[33] Her mother's father was named Candido and her father's father was José, so she was named Candida José, though she called herself Candace. Her sister, Linda Diana, was named after her grandfather's sister, Hermilinda, and her mother, Diana. Her brother was given the name Patrick Jonathan after his father, Patricio, and his father's best friend, Jonathan. After the baptism at church, births were commonly celebrated with a family gathering at home.[34]

---

[28] After Tony Montour, Sr.'s mother died while giving birth to him, the family created a composite photo showing him as a baby with his mother before she became pregnant ("Created photo, Tony Montour, Sr.").

[29] Bernal, Dora, interview, 1978.

[30] Ortega, Roseann Chavez, interview, 1986.

[31] Maestas, Roy, interview, 1978.

[32] For photos, see "Shirley Roybal at baptism" and "Angie and Ray Perez at christening."

[33] Arroyo, Candace, interview, 1977.

[34] "Martinez, Juan and Josephine; Marcella Diaz, biography."

Illus. 1.11. *Children at a birthday party*

How birthdays were handled varied between families and over time. Virginia Madrigal Martinez said that her grandparents, who had come to Boulder County from Mexico in 1910, had been given their saint's names at birth.[35] They celebrated their birthdays with a big party. "There was music, by my grandfather and his sons, good food, excellent wine, singing and dancing. Everyone had a good time. I will never forget those gatherings." Three of the older Latinas/os living in the Water + Goss Streets area of Boulder (Mrs. Esther Maes, E. E. Bernal, and Roy Maestas) had birthdays on the same day, and their families would get together.[36] After the mid-twentieth century, parents were increasingly likely to put on birthday parties for children with other young guests.

In a long interview done in 1976, Teresa Alvarez, who was then 79 years old, talked about several aspects of raising young children.[37] In the 1910s-1930s, a time when baby bottles and infant formula were rare and expensive, nearly all mothers breast-fed their babies. Teresa said she had plenty of milk for all of her nine babies that lived past infancy except for one, whom she bottle fed. She usually had enough milk to help feed the babies of other women who lived near them in the mining camps

---

[35] "Madrigal family of Boulder, biographies."
[36] "Maestas, Pedro (Roy), Ruby, and Abe, biography." For this neighborhood, see Ch. 2B below.
[37] Alvarez, Teresa, interview, 1976, for this paragraph and the next.

Illus. 1.12. Two toddlers in a wash tub

around Lafayette but did not have sufficient milk themselves. Teresa normally continued breast-feeding her babies until they were about two years old, when she began to give them well cooked oatmeal or mashed potatoes mixed with milk. Keeping babies clean was a special challenge if the dwelling lacked water and heat, though conditions improved for most families later.[38]

The next step was toilet training. Teresa, who lived in housing with no indoor water or toilets when her children were small, described how she did it. She started with a little potty, a wooden seat with a bowl under it that could be used inside and then emptied into the outhouse. As the child grew older and larger, her husband would put a board across the seat in the outhouse to make it safe. Eventually the child could use the regular outhouse seat without danger of falling in.[39]

As children moved past the toddler stage, urban ones had more chances to interact with youngsters outside their own families than did rural ones. Younger children in Longmont enjoyed playing with their friends close to home or sometimes going swimming.[40] Older ones in

[38] See also "Angie Perez bathing baby."

[39] Cf. "Two girls in an outhouse."

[40] E.g., "Three young children playing in yard" and "Children swimming in Longmont." For below, see Ch. 4C below.

Boulder played pick-up ballgames in a nearby vacant lot. By the 1950s, teens were becoming increasingly involved in social or athletic activities with their Latino and sometimes Anglo peers. Nearly all Latino children living in Boulder County appear to have attended school.[41] While some dropped out during or at the end of elementary school to start working, a growing number continued into secondary education. By their early teens, however, even those who were still in school were expected to contribute to the family's income by working during the summers and/ or in the afternoons and weekends.

During the early part of the century, and for rural households into the 1960s, families had an important role in introducing young people to suitable partners and giving approval to marriages. Virginia Madrigal Martinez wrote in 2012 about how young people in her grandparents' generations chose their spouse.

> Usually a young woman picked a young man who was a member of their family's friends. The parents played a big part in the couple's relationship. My grandmother married at 14 years of age. It seems young, but they learned how to cook and take care of their brothers and sisters at an early age. When my grandparents wanted to get married, he had to ask her father for her hand in marriage. After two weeks, my grandfather would get his answer.[42]

In that pattern, parents kept a close eye on their daughters' social lives. Teresa Alvarez's husband was unusually strict. When her daughters were growing up in Lafayette in the 1930s, her husband did not want them to date at all.[43] A boy needed to park his car in the back alley, and once the girl had checked that her father was not looking, she would slip out to join him. If the couple later decided to marry, the boy would come to ask Teresa's husband for permission. The father was upset that they had been going out without his knowledge, but in the end he always said yes.

By the later 1940s and 1950s, urban Latinas/os in their teens and early twenties had more freedom. Now they commonly met possible marriage partners through their friends or at dances. Linda Arroyo-Holmstrom said that her dad, Pat, met his future wife, Diana, thanks to a good friend of his who was dating a friend of Diana's. Pat's friend thought,

[41] See Ch. 6C below.
[42] "Madrigal family of Boulder, biographies."
[43] Alvarez, Teresa, interview, 1976.

"Boy, Diana would be the perfect woman for Pat, and so he introduced my father to my mother, and that's when they started dating."[44] Parents nevertheless maintained some control over their daughters' social lives. Marcella Diaz, who grew up in Boulder's Water + Goss Streets community in the later 1940s and 1950s, remembered that "the girls were allowed to date, but the boys had to come to the door and ask for permission to take us out. If the boy was courteous and respectful, then permission was granted and a curfew was given. The curfew was usually 10:00 p.m. If we returned late, the curfew for the next date was changed to an earlier time."[45]

Starting in the post-World War II period, when many young women living in towns had at least part-time jobs, their employment offered a wider range of social contacts. Mary Gonzales first met her future husband, Richard Tafoya, in the late 1940s, when she was 14 years old.[46] Seven years later, she was frying hamburgers one day at the City Café, owned by her dad, Alex Gonzales. Richard, who had just returned from fighting in Korea, came into the café and saw a picture of Mary that Alex had put up on the wall.

> Richard said, "I know that girl."
>
> Dad was always suspicious and wanted to know how Richard knew me. Richard explained that we had picked beans together.
>
> "Well, she's in the kitchen now," Dad told him.
>
> Richard came back to the kitchen to talk with me. He was really good-looking and he had dimples. He stayed and stayed.
>
> "You have to go now," I told him. "You'll get me in trouble."
>
> I had to sneak out to see Richard. We'd meet at Collyer Park. I was like Cinderella: I had to get home by midnight, before Dad got home from working the swing shift at the mine.[47]

Even in Boulder, however, where some young Latinas worked full-time for a few years before marriage, we see little evidence of the gender developments found in cities like Los Angeles and El Paso during the 1940s and 1950s.[48] There second-generation Mexican women, some of whom had jobs in defense-related industries, used their own incomes

---

[44] Arroyo-Holmstrom, Linda, interview, 2013.
[45] "Martinez, Juan and Josephine; Marcella Diaz, biography."
[46] Tafoya, Mary Gonzales, interview, 2009, for this and below.
[47] Ibid.
[48] Alvarez, *Power of the Zoot*, esp. chs. 3-4, Catherine Ramirez, *Woman in the Zoot Suit*, esp. chs. 1-2, and Escobedo, *From Coveralls to Zoot Suits*, esp. ch. 4.

to support new leisure activities: buying clothes and makeup, wearing distinctive hair styles, going out with a group of other girls to enjoy jazz music and jitterbug dancing, and dating men with little if any supervision. Some formed gangs that donned Zoot Suit or *pachuca* clothing.[49] These behaviors blurred familiar definitions of masculinity and femininity and conflicted with the expectations for appropriate female behavior held by their older relatives and perhaps by prospective husbands. Recent scholarship argues that as these urban women negotiated the resulting gender tension, they created a new model of Mexican American womanhood, one distinct from both earlier Latino cultural patterns and the dominant Anglo world around them.[50]

In Boulder, however, young Latinas remained more conservative, in part because their families thought it important to demonstrate respectability as a way of promoting acceptance by Anglo culture.[51] Further, although some young people had Anglo friends of the same sex, they do not seem to have engaged in inter-racial or inter-ethnic dating, as sometimes occurred in California.[52] Nearly all Boulder County Latinas/os married people of similar ethnic background until later in the century.

Marriage was a major event, often commemorated in a formal photograph of the couple or the wedding party.[53] Some undated but historic photos kept by Longmont families in the 1980s show traditional

---

[49] It often included a relatively short shirt or long draped slacks, a jacket of finger-tip length, bobby socks or fishnet stockings, dark lipstick and/or other makeup, and pompadoured, upswept hair (Catherine Ramirez, *Woman in the Zoot Suit*, p. xii and ch.1, Escobedo, *From Coveralls to Zoot Suits*, pp. 9 and 11, and Alvarez, *Power of the Zoot*, p. 88).

[50] See note 47 above.

[51] See Vol. I, Ch. 5C. The first indication of distinctive Mexican American clothing and body art in the Boulder County materials comes from 1987: "Cholos y Cholas." For atypical Boulder women who enjoyed an active social life in California during the 1940s and 1950s, see Rose Olivas and Dora Bernal, below.

[52] Escobedo, *From Coveralls to Zoot Soots*, ch. 4. Interracial marriage was banned in Colorado until 1957, except for southern areas of the state that had formerly belonged to Mexico (Abbott et al., *Colorado*, p. 353). The racial definition of Latinas/os with respect to marriage was ill defined.

[53] See, e.g. "Joseph and Sabina Cortez," "Wedding of John S. and Tillie Chavez, 1940," "Edward John Tafoya and Delia Mary Vargas, wedding commemoration," "Wedding of Emma Gomez and John Martinez," "Wedding of John Anthony Rivera and Marilyn Martinez Rivera," "Wedding of Clofes Luisa Mondragon and Juan Francisco Archuleta," "Wedding of Becky and Dave Ortega," and "Martinez, Fabricio, and Letia Madrid on wedding day."

Illus. 1.13. Small group at a traditional wedding, with guitar

weddings in New Mexico and southern Colorado.[54] Many other images document later weddings. Marriages were usually celebrated with a religious service, even if it was not legally necessary. When Roy Maestas married around 1930, he was working at a coal mine in southern Colorado and could not leave his job to go to church.[55] But when the couple moved to Lafayette in the late 1930s, they had a (belated) religious wedding.

If at all possible, couples wanted to throw some kind of a party to celebrate their marriage. Even if they were living in poverty, they would save or borrow money or ask for contributions from friends in order to make a gathering possible. Teve Ojeda, who moved to Erie in 1926, described how wedding festivities there were financed.[56] She said that by custom the bride's parents paid for the marriage ceremony, while the groom covered the cost of her dress and other accessories. The maid of honor hosted a wedding breakfast for the bride and paid for the cake. Everyone involved in the wedding contributed money to rent a hall and pay a band for the dance.

Among some established Boulder families, planning and saving for a wedding could take six months to a year. The event itself might extend

[54] See also Vol. I, Illus. 2.4.
[55] Maestas, Roy, interview, 1978.
[56] Adelfang, ed., *Erie*, p. 41. Erie lies a few miles NE of Lafayette.

Illus. 1.14. Garcia wedding photo, 1913

Illus. 1.15. Wedding, Jennie Razo and Richard Romero, 1950

over two days: dinner the day before, the wedding the next morning at church, then a reception and dance later that afternoon and evening. Marcella Diaz described her wedding in 1959, which started with a marriage ceremony at Sacred Heart Church, to which the family members of the bride and groom plus local friends were invited.[57] It was followed by a reception and dance at home, with food prepared by the extended family and open to anyone who wanted to attend. The dance at her wedding included a religious component as well. "The parents of both the bride and the groom stood over the kneeling newly-weds, and said a special prayer and blessed the couple. The parents' blessing culminated in them making the sign of the cross over the bride and groom. I always thought this a very special part of my wedding." By the later 1970s, some couples were celebrating their 50th wedding anniversaries with large family parties and/or renewing their vows in church, likewise recorded in photos.[58]

Funerals and the associated customs formed the final transition. They involved the whole family: there was no attempt to shield children from the reality of death and burial. Virginia Madrigal Martinez said that her grandparents took her to several funerals when she was a little girl living in Boulder in the late 1930s.[59] "In those days the wake was held at the person's home. All his friends gathered around him and told stories about the 'deceased.' The women of the family would cry and howl over the body. After the crying stopped, food and drink was served and it turned into a big party. The next day the funeral was held at the church; he then was taken to the cemetery." Marcella Diaz commented, "Since most people died at home, in big families *la muerte* was no stranger. We didn't think of death as happening only to someone else.... As children we were taken to the *velorio* (wake) for the *difunto* (the deceased). We were taught to pay our last respects and express our *pesame* (condolences), and to accompany the casket to the cemetery."[60]

Lowering the casket into the grave was an important ritual, because everyone present threw a little earth onto it. As late as 1977, Susie Gomez Chacon said that Latinas/os were objecting to the practice

[57] "Martinez, Juan and Josephine; Marcella Diaz, biography."
[58] "Wedding and 50th Wedding Anniversary of Tony Montour, Sr., and Julia Rodriguez Montour," "Mr. and Mrs. Alex Gonzales's 50th wedding anniversary," "Delia and Edward Tafoya's 50th wedding anniversary," and "Delia and Edward Tafoya, Renewal of vows."
[59] "Madrigal family of Boulder, biographies."
[60] "Martinez, Juan and Josephine; Marcella Diaz, biography."

Illus. 1.16. *Petra and Rita Quintana tending a grave, Longmont*

among some morticians of asking people to leave the cemetery before that happened.[61] They said, "'No, I'm going to stay until that casket goes down, because we still have dirt for the casket.' The grave was then maintained by family members.

A death in the family was traditionally followed by a period of mourning. Marcella Diaz commented that when she was growing up with her conservative grandparents, the immediate and extended family of the deceased were expected to wear "black or dark colors for periods, as imposed by patriarchs/matriarchs [within the family], which could be up to one year. There were also other restrictions imposed. No singing, no music or such."[62] Mourning became less extensive later. The death of one spouse could leave the survivor without skills and resources, a need to which various senior service organizations in the county were responding by the 1960s.[63]

Early cemetery listings for Longmont, Lafayette, and Boulder imply that not all Latino residents were buried in official graveyards with stones giving their name and date of death. If we compare the number of people with Latino surnames included in the list of Lafayette gravestones

[61] Chacon, Susie, interview, 1977.
[62] "Martinez, Juan and Josephine; Marcella Diaz, biography."
[63] E.g., "Sally Martinez as an Elderly Widow."

prior to the 1960s with the total number of Latinas/os living in the town during those decades, there are fewer recorded burials than we should have seen.[64] The number of cemetery burials in Longmont is somewhat too low, as is Boulder's prior to the 1930s. People who did not live near a church may have been unable to arrange for formal burial; infants were probably especially likely to have been buried close to where the family was living at the time. Even town dwellers may not have been able to pay for a cemetery plot, or at least not for a grave marker with full information.

Latino families displayed great resiliency across the generations discussed here. The conception of marriage as an economic partnership for the good of the whole family, promoting the well-being of the children, often trumped a desire to preserve customary gender and generational roles. Many fathers in Boulder County adjusted to the increase in formal education, which might mean that their children were better able to function within the Anglo world than they were.[65] Many husbands accommodated themselves to female employment outside the home, including positions that put women into regular contact with other men or brought public visibility.[66] There is, however, some evidence of inter-generational tension, especially between immigrant parents/grandparents and younger people who had become more acculturated to Anglo ways through schooling and jobs.[67] Latino families were generally able to continue providing warmth and backing for their members precisely because of their flexibility. One of the legacies left by earlier Latinas/os to people living in Boulder County in the early twenty-first century was the emotional and practical support given by strong but adaptable families.[68]

[64] For the minimum number of adult residents, see Vol. I, App. 1.2.
[65] See Ch. 6 below.
[66] See Vol. I, Chs. 5A and 6C.
[67] See, e.g., Vol. I, Chs. 5C and 7A.
[68] Some contemporary Latino families, however, had been disrupted by immigration: see the lives of the interns described in the Epilogue, below.

Chapter 2

Housing and Neighborhoods

Many aspects of Latino life occurred within the dwellings in which families lived and—for urban residents—the neighborhoods that surrounded them. Individual houses, some of which were of minimal quality, were commonly the setting for family gatherings, social and cultural events, and religious practice. The physical context might be extended for people in towns to include other families living near them, though the degree of "neighborliness" or sense of community among them varied. The unique interactive computer-based maps prepared by the BCLHP, which display Latino-surnamed households in our three towns in each decade between 1904 or 1916 and 1975, allow us to see where families and students lived and how Latinas/os gradually spread out within those communities.

A. Housing

The buildings that sheltered Boulder County's Latino families between 1900 and 1980 covered a wide range in terms of size and comfort, depending in part upon what kind of work their residents did and whether they were located in rural areas (farms or mining camps) or in towns. Although much of this housing earlier in the century was very basic, and sometimes clearly substandard to modern eyes, it gradually improved over time for most Latinas/os except migrant workers.[1]

During the first part of the century, housing for married men differed from that for single men. When Roy Maestas was working in coal mines in the late 1920s and 1930s, his family lived in little wooden houses in the camps set up around the mines.[2] The houses were heated with coal and wood, with no toilets; at first they had coal oil lamps, but electricity

---

[1] For housing for migrant families, see Vol. I, Ch. 6B.
[2] Maestas, Roy, interview, 1978, and see, e.g., "Houses in camp, Industrial Mine."

was introduced later. Some camps had only tents as living places or used them as bath houses for the miners.[3] Unmarried miners generally lived in boarding houses, where they slept and ate their meals. At least in Erie, there were separate houses for the different nationalities, with cooks who knew how to prepare the kind of food the residents liked.[4] Unmarried agricultural workers too might be boarders. When Teresa Alvarez was orphaned at age 13, she went to live with a foster family near Fort Collins.[5] Her foster parents contracted workers for farm owners and took in boarders, one of whom Teresa later married.

For regular farm laborers—who were hired either for the season (spring through early fall) or for a full year—some kind of housing was generally provided by their employer. Mr. and Mrs. E. E. Bernal were beet workers on various farms around southeastern Boulder County from 1919 until 1934. When interviewed in 1977, Mrs. Bernal said that most of the houses they had lived in were "no good."[6] They were made of wood and about to fall down, because the farmers did not repair them or give the tenants materials to fix them up. They were also very cold, with heat coming only from the wood burning stove used for cooking. There was no electricity, just oil lamps.

Dora Bernal, who later married E. E.'s brother, spent summers in the early 1920s with her parents and siblings on beet farms in this area. In the summer of 1923 they had a nice house that the farmer had previously lived in himself; it had six rooms that they shared with only one other family.[7] But the following year "we were given a shack of one small room, or let's say a room and a half. Because the room was about 12 by 14 feet, and the other was about the size of my kitchen, about 6 by 8 feet. . . . That room was made out of wooden pieces picked up from a train track." The building was also terribly cold when they arrived in March.

Conditions for farm workers had not improved much by the 1940s and 1950s, even if they were year-round employees.[8] Virginia Maestas's parents and five children moved to a different farm in Boulder County each year during the early 1940s, living in whatever accommodations were provided by their employers. The houses she remembers generally had a kitchen (which functioned as a living room, dining room, kitchen,

---

[3] Martinez, Sally, and others, interview, 1990.
[4] Adelfang, ed., *Erie*, p. 40.
[5] Alvarez, Teresa, interview, 1976.
[6] Bernal, Mr. and Mrs. Emerenciano, interview, 1977.
[7] Bernal, Dora, interview, 1978, translated from her Spanish statement.
[8] "Farm family and Secundino Herrera in front of home."

and laundry room) plus two other rooms, used only for sleeping.[9] When they moved in 1945 to the Stengel farm east of Boulder, on 75th Street at Baseline Road, they lived in "a little shack" about two blocks south of the main farmhouse. Secundino Herrera came to Longmont in 1951 with his wife, two sons, and eight daughters. Their house on Lloyd Dickens' ranch was a shack, "like a stable for calves."[10] Although it was common at the time for farmers to provide housing, Secundino disliked that arrangement: "I didn't want to continue to live under the fat thumb of the ranchers who were so unjust." So, "the first chance I got, I rented a house on a monthly basis, so now I had a place of my own and started saving to build my own house. I found it very nice to make my own decisions on where I wanted to work instead of being restricted on one farm."[11]

When Emma Gomez Martinez began working for the Office of Economic Opportunity in 1965 as a Neighborhood Aide and Counselor, she found that while the housing of most poor Latino families in the county was deplorable, agricultural workers faced even greater challenges.

> Families working in fields had housing that was worse than where the farmers stored their machines. They lived behind the nice barns in small, falling down shelters. There were either broken windows or no windows, and mattresses on the floor. They had to use outhouses and had to bring water from the wells. Electricity? One bulb strung from the machinery barn.[12]

People living in housing provided by their employers had no security if they became unable to work, even if they sustained an injury on the job. In 1958, Joe and Lou Cardenas had been field workers for 13 years on the Mayeda farm in Longmont.[13] Joe worked right through those years, going from pay of 35 cents per hour to 45 cents; Lou signed on once their children were a little older, receiving 10 cents per hour less than her husband. They and their five children lived in a house on the farm until Joe was injured. As Lou later described,

We were having supper when Johnny Mayeda came over. He said,

---

[9] Maestas, Virginia, interview, 1978.

[10] Herrera, Secundino, interview, 1979.

[11] Herrera, Secundino, interview, c. 1987.

[12] "Martinez, Emma Gomez, letter to her children."

[13] Cardenas, Lou, interview, c. 1987. The Mayedas were one of the Japanese families who had come to Longmont several generations before as sugar beet workers but gradually bought land of their own (see Vol. I, Ch. 3A).

"Joe, I know you got hurt working on the beets on the topper, but since you can't work anymore I think it would be best if you moved out. We need the house by next weekend." So here we were, looking for a house all over Longmont. We couldn't find one. So we went to Mead and we found a little shack, but it was okay for the time being.[14]

Joe took a job at the turkey plant and later at another farm.

Although agricultural workers and miners generally regarded houses in the towns as better than accommodations in the fields and camps, most urban homes were small one-story buildings, often poorly constructed and with minimal conveniences. When Roy Maestas's family moved to Boulder in the late 1930s, he was pleased that the little house they rented had electricity and indoor water.[15] As late as the 1960s, Mike Romero was laying down the first wood floor in his old house in Lafayette, which had previously had only a dirt floor.[16] Another kind of modest housing was erected in Boulder after World War II, when the City put up quonset huts on land owned by the school district, near the corner of Water and 21st Streets, to house veterans and their families.[17] Lafayette's Lions Club spearheaded a project in 1954 to build up to 50 new but affordable homes on the southwest side of town.[18] The prefabricated houses, with central gas heating and good insulation, were FHA financed, selling for $6,000 for two bedrooms and $6,500 for three bedrooms. As of 1989, some of the original owners, including Dave and Becky Ortega, still resided in the same homes.

Early Latinas/os were eager to own their own houses and worked hard to save up enough money to make that possible. After their marriage in 1927, Donaciana and Alfredo Arguello moved to Boulder County from the Trinidad/Walsenburg area.[19] They and their many children lived in mining camps in the winters and in farm buildings during the summer. In 1947, one month before Donaciana gave birth to her thirteenth baby (the only one born in a hospital), Alfredo died, leaving her on her own with the children. As their daughter Cecelia later explained,

[14] Cardenas, Lou, interview, c. 1987.
[15] Maestas, Roy, interview, 1978.
[16] Jim Hutchison, conversation with Marjorie McIntosh, Jan. 7, 2014.
[17] "Biographical sketch, Emma Gomez Martinez." Water Street was later redeveloped as Canyon Boulevard. See Vol. I, Ch. 5C.
[18] *Lafayette, Colorado*, T66.
[19] "Arguello, Alfredo and Donaciana and family, biography," for this and below.

> There was a black-and-white ceramic piggy bank in which my father was saving money to buy a house someday. When he died from complications of diabetes and tuberculosis, there was enough money to buy a house for $500 on Marshall Place in east Longmont. The house only had two rooms and a basement (more like a fruit cellar). It had an outside toilet, and the kitchen was housed in a building separate from the house.

Later some friends donated their labor to extend the house, which then included a large kitchen, back porch, small bedroom, and indoor toilet.

The stories told about early arrivals to the Water + Goss Streets area of Boulder demonstrate how much owning a family home mattered. Benjamin and Mary Mercedes Madrigal moved to Boulder in 1931.[20] Because of the Great Depression, Benjamin had trouble finding work at first, so he took employment through the Works Progress Administration: putting up buildings on the university campus, constructing an outdoor theater on Flagstaff Mountain, and building roads in Boulder and the mountains. In 1936, he was hired by the Western States Cutlery factory, and four years later, the Madrigals were able to buy a house near Goss Street. Juan and Clofes Archuleta moved their family from southern Colorado to Boulder in 1932.[21] Juan, a former coal miner, worked as a stonemason for the university and at various quarries in Lyons, north of the town; Clofes was at home with their eight children. In 1945, their savings plus life insurance after their son Arthur was killed in action in World War II enabled them to buy a house on Water Street.[22] When E. E. Bernal and Roy Maestas brought their families to Boulder, they both rented initially but later purchased their own homes.[23] Linda Arroyo-Holmstrom's grandparents moved to Boulder in 1945 and were able to buy a house quite soon.[24] Her grandfather, who was a miner during the winters, did handyman jobs during the summers. One of the people he worked for was an attorney in Boulder, who helped him with the process of purchasing a house at 2040 Pearl Street. Linda's parents later bought the house behind it, across the back alley, at 2041 Walnut, where they were still living in 2013.

An occasional Latino family was able to buy multiple buildings and

---

[20] "Madrigal family of Boulder, biographies."
[21] "Archuleta family history."
[22] See Vol. I, Ch. 5B.
[23] Bernal, Mr. and Mrs. Emerenciano, interview, 1977, and Maestas, Roy, interview, 1978.
[24] Arroyo-Holmstrom, Linda, interview, 2013.

use them to generate income. Pete Saragosa (originally Pedro Zaragoza) came to Boulder from Zacatecas with his two brothers in the 1910s.[25] They soon started buying property in the town: first at 19th and Water Streets, and then two "ranches" on the western end of what are now Alpine and Pearl Streets. The ranches housed their families and supported them: they raised animals and grew vegetables and fruit for sale. Between 1919 and 1926, Pete, who was financially savvy, got cash through a series of mortgages (on real estate and personal goods), enabling him to buy additional property.[26] After his death, however, his widow was unable to hang on to the real estate, and by 1946 she had sold all of it. In the 1950s and early 1960s, John S. Chavez and his wife Tillie owned a house at 741 Pearl Street in Boulder.[27] It had been divided into apartments, which they rented out except for the one in which they lived with their two children.

The gradual improvement in housing over time, and the benefits of living in a town, are illustrated by the experience of Juan and Josephine Martinez. They were originally from northern New Mexico but had to leave their homes due to poverty in the mid-1920s.[28] At first, they travelled around that area and southern Colorado as migrant farm workers, taking whatever employment they could find, while living in a covered wagon. During the late 1920s and early 1930s, they spent most winters in Romeo, a little town at the southern end of the San Luis Valley "where the snow was constant, deep, houses so cold at night that their buckets of water would be solid ice in the mornings." Their last child (one of the eight who lived) was born in 1946 in Ordway, Colorado, on the plains east of Pueblo, in a two-room barn on the farm where the family was working. When that job ended, Juan had to take a position elsewhere as a sheepherder, living in a small trailer with only a dog and a horse to keep him company. Josephine moved the children into the nearby town of Sugar City—a community built by the National Beet Sugar Company—where they lived at first in a two-room shack owned by a Mexican immigrant who later became their son-in-law. Within two

---

[25] Leslie Ogeda, conversation with Marjorie McIntosh, April 12, 2013, and Gonzales, Doris, interview, 2013.

[26] "Saragosa, Pete, property records."

[27] "Chavez family home." For Chavez's job at Rocky Flats Nuclear Weapons Plant, see Vol. I, Illus. 6.5; for his positions at Sacred Heart of Jesus Church, see Ch. 5C below.

[28] "Martinez, Juan and Josephine; Marcella Diaz, biography" for this paragraph.

years, Juan and Josephine were able to buy a two-room house of their own in Sugar City. In 1954 the parents and four children who were still at home moved to Goss Street in Boulder to be near a married daughter who had health problems and needed care. Initially they lived in the basement of a rented house, then in an upstairs apartment. Both parents were now working (Juan as a grounds man at the University, Josephine cleaning houses), and in another two years they were able to buy a house on Water Street, where they remained for many years.

Families sometimes shared housing. Latino families were reluctant to place their older relatives into an institution, even if they could afford the cost. They preferred (and still prefer) to help their parents keep on living in their own homes for as long as possible, giving them the practical assistance they need; if an older person required regular care, close relatives would generally take him or her into their household. For younger people too, sharing a dwelling might be necessary, at least temporarily. Eleanor Montour, when she was leading a walking tour in 2013 of places in Lafayette that have been important to Latinas/os, pointed out that her grandparents' house and many others had a smaller building in the back.[29] It was used by young family members when they first married, by relatives who had lost their jobs, or by people who were sick or injured and needed to be looked after. Tony Gomez's dad came to Longmont around 1945, where he worked for the Great Western Sugar factory in the section where they boiled the beets.[30] Early in their marriage, he and his wife lived in a little house on Marshall Street that Tony's grandfather had given to two of his sons, located behind the grandparents' own house. Later Tony's family moved into the larger house with the older couple. After Pat and Diana Arroyo's wedding, they stayed with his parents until they could find and afford a place of their own; when Abe and Virginia Maestas and their daughter returned to Boulder after he finished his college degree in Pueblo, they lived at first with his parents.[31]

Joint housing was also common for new immigrants.[32] When Olga Melendez Cordero's Mexican father and uncle returned to Longmont with their families around 1967-8, having previously come as *braceros*,

[29] On July 29, 2013; segments from the videographed tour were used by Ana Gonzalez Dorta for her film ("Lafayette, film of places of historical importance"), but this part was not.

[30] Gomez, Tony, interview, 2009. For the sugar factory, see Vol. I, Ch. 3C.

[31] Arroyo-Holmstrom, Linda, interview, 2013; Maestas, Virginia, interview, 1978.

[32] That pattern remained true into the twenty-first century: see the Epilogue below.

they rented a little house at 15 East 5th Avenue.[33] Olga's parents with their five girls lived in the basement; her uncle and aunt lived on the main floor with their six children. The two families wanted to stay near each other, so when they had saved up enough money, they bought that house plus the one next door.

B. Neighborhood Communities and the Interactive Maps

The extent to which Latinas/os lived in neighborhoods filled with family and friends from their own culture varied between our three towns. Each had one or more areas in which Latinas/os clustered. Characterized by inexpensive houses located near a railway line, these were generally regarded as undesirable neighborhoods, filled with the families of manual laborers, a class-based definition. Housing was not actively segregated by race or ethnicity, however, for people from different backgrounds lived side-by-side, and some Latinas/os found housing elsewhere in the towns. While a decision to settle in an area that included other Latinas/os may have been voluntary for some families, it is likely that real estate agents during the later 1940s, 1950s, and 1960s discouraged Latinas/os from moving into the "better" neighborhoods where many Anglos lived. The observation that few of Boulder County's urban Latinas/os lived in areas surrounded by people solely of their own background suggests that towns located on the edge of the borderlands had different housing patterns than the more homogeneous *barrios* of major cities of the Southwest.[34]

We have quantitative and visual evidence about the location of Latino households in the three towns thanks to information from *Polk's City Directories*, which the BCLHP analyzed once per decade between 1904 and 1975.[35] Volunteers entered data into spreadsheets about those households whose head had a Latino surname, or any other name known to belong to a local Latino family (like Blazón and Montour).

---

[33] Cordero, Olga Melendez, interview, 2009. For the *Braceros* program, see Vol. I, Ch. 5A.

[34] Alamillo, however, describes neighborhoods in the southern California citrus area in which Italian and Mexican immigrants lived side-by-side, despite the nearby presence of a largely Mexican *barrio* (*Making Lemonade*, pp. 48-54).

[35] *Polk's City Directories*, available in Boulder County's public libraries, list adult residents of each town by street address and give the occupations and employers of some of them. For this project, volunteers entered information into databases about those households headed by people with Hispanic surnames, using as sample years 1904,

While the resulting lists are certainly not entirely complete, they provide invaluable information about general patterns. Interactive maps were then prepared from those spreadsheets.[36] Households that contain students are shown in red, to distinguish growth of resident Latino families from the increasing number of students coming from elsewhere and living in the community only temporarily. A second set of maps for Longmont only are based on the U.S. Census records for 1920, 1930, and 1940. Rebecca Chavez's analysis includes every household that had any Latino-surnamed residents or people born in Mexico.[37]

The interactive maps are in one respect somewhat misleading visually, because the base maps against which the markers are displayed show streets as they existed in 2014. Since each of the towns was far smaller prior to 1950 than it was to become later, the apparent absence of Latino households from some areas may simply mean that those subdivisions had not yet been developed. That problem is illustrated by the interactive maps for Lafayette, which seem to show that the town's Latino families were concentrated within a fairly limited area through the mid-1960s. But during those decades, Lafayette's entire residential neighborhood was confined to an area stretching from Bermont Avenue on the west to South Burlington on the east, and from Elm Street on the northeast, a few blocks beyond Baseline Road, to Emma Street on the south. Hence it was not just that Latinas/os lived there, everyone did. We will look at the residential layout of Latinas/os in each town separately.

In Lafayette, which had no more than around 2,000 residents until 1960, the neighborhood where Latinas/os lived was bisected by a railroad line for the coal mines that ran diagonally across it.[38] Most Latinas/os

1916 (using *Polk's Boulder County Directory*), 1926, 1936, 1946, 1955, 1965, and 1975. The resulting figures are minimum numbers, though coverage is fuller in the later decades. The *Directories* probably missed some people and did not include true migrant workers; this analysis may have failed to recognize some Hispanic names and could not spot any Latinas who married a man with a non-Latino surname, though inter-ethnic marriage was rare in this area until around 1970. The Boulder maps begin in 1904; the Lafayette and Longmont ones in 1916.

[36] The maps are accessible from the BCLHP's website, bocolatinohistory.colorado.edu, under "Interactive City Maps," and will not be individually cited here.

[37] Although these displays are potentially more complete in terms of their coverage of people, a number of Latinas/os included in the Censuses could not be mapped: those listed without a specific street address or described as living along a Rural Route. Chavez's spreadsheets ("U.S. Census Records for Longmont," 1920, 1930, and 1940) were prepared for her thesis, "Making Them Count." The maps are available on the BCLHP's website, under "Interactive City Maps."

lived in small and often poorly built houses, but their yards were large enough to provide space for vegetable and flower gardens. Most of the residents were current or former coal miners, though they came from several different ethnic backgrounds.[39] At the beginning of the twentieth century, many were immigrants from eastern or southeastern Europe. Serbs and Bulgarians were then joined by people from southern Italy and by new arrivals from Mexico, New Mexico, and southern Colorado.

In 2013 Eleanor Montour described the core Lafayette neighborhood where she grew up the 1940s and 1950s. "Many of the men that my grandfather worked with and that we lived around were Italians. So I grew up in a neighborhood that was both Latino and Italian. It was a very loud neighborhood. We all talked very loud, very rapidly, very quickly."[40] They shared not only their languages but also their foods. At Christmas, Eleanor's grandmother would get all her family together to make tamales, and they would buy red wine for their dinner from the Italian family next door and salad from an Italian family across the street. Eleanor recalled those interactions as "enriching, both monetarily and socially."

Sociability among Lafayette's Latinas/os normally occurred within their extended families or with close friends living nearby. Eleanor Montour pointed out that when she was a child living at 206 East Chester Street, her grandparents' house was across the street; their good friends the Gomezes lived in that block too.[41] Eleanor's aunt and great-aunt were in the 300 block of East Chester, as were their friends the Ortegas, and an uncle lived two blocks further along. These living arrangements provided "safety in numbers, being close to family so they could help each other."

Lafayette's Latino neighborhood had several other good features. It offered easy access to the Catholic Church, important for those families who were regular attenders, and it included several small stores that were willing to give credit. This was important to mining families, for

---

[38] See static "Map of Lafayette in 1906? (part 1)" and "Map of Lafayette in 1918 (part 1)."

[39] See Vol. I, Ch. 3B.

[40] Montour, Eleanor, interview, 2013.

[41] "Lafayette, film of places of historical importance." As that video displays, some of the older houses had been replaced by mobile homes by 2013. For a tour of Lafayette set up in the late 1990s, see "Lafayette's historic walking trail," "Walking tours to highlight Lafayette's historic buildings," and "Dedication of Native and Hispanic Heritage Walk."

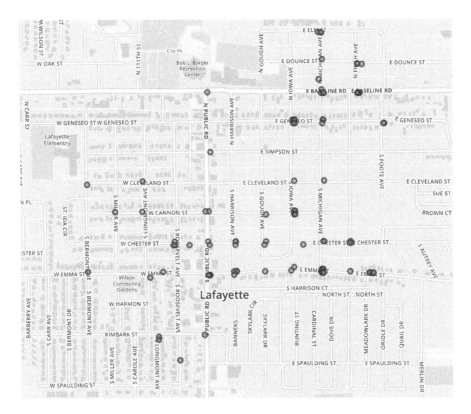

Illus. 2.1. *Screen shot of interactive map showing Latino-headed households in Lafayette, 1955*

work was available only during the colder months, and even then, paychecks were given only twice each month. If cash ran low, many families relied upon their good reputations with local merchants to continue buying essential items, especially food. Eleanor Montour talked warmly about the stores that gave her family credit when she was a child: Hale's Groceries and Joe's and O'Dell's Markets.[42]

The interactive maps show that in the mid-1910s and mid-1920s, few Latino households were listed in Lafayette, but the number had started to increase by 1936, including the beginnings of the East Chester/East Emma Street cluster described by Montour. The density of Latinas/os in that core area rose gradually across the next three decades. A turning point is visible in the 1970s, however, with many Latinas/os still living in the old neighborhood but now a movement out into newer subdivisions

[42] "Lafayette, film of places of historical importance."

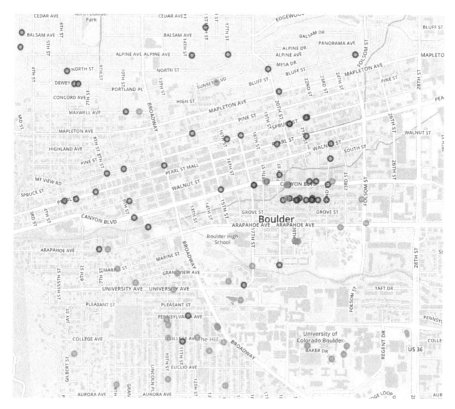

Illus. 2.2. *Screen shot of interactive map showing Latino-headed households in Central Boulder, 1955*

as well.

In Boulder, the area we have titled "the Water + Goss Streets" neighborhood included Water Street (later redeveloped as Canyon Boulevard) on the north and Goss Street one block south; it extended east-west from 17th Street to 24th Street (later re-worked as Folsom).[43] Latino families living in the five blocks north of Water Street, as far as Mapleton, were sometimes included in the sociability that marked the core area. The Water + Goss Streets community was located near Boulder Creek, with a railway line running down the middle of Water Street, and its little houses were inexpensive to rent or buy. Although it lay at the base of University Hill, its residents had few interactions with the academic world until the late 1960s, except sometimes as employees.

---

[43] For the appearance of this area in the late 1970s, see "Boulder's Chicano Community, 1979 film"; for 2013, when few of the original houses were left, see "Boulder, film of places of historical importance."

This was an ethnically and racially mixed but sociai. community from the mid-1930s into the 1960s. During nineteenth century the area had been where Boulder's few ⌐. Americans lived.[44] By the 1940s, Water + Goss Streets included remaining blacks and some Italians and Anglos as well as the Latinas/oↄ who were now moving in. Whereas only four Latino families had come to the Water + Goss Streets area in the 1910s and 1920s and another six in the 1930s, the numbers rose thereafter.[45] During the 1940s, 16 Latino families came in hopes of a better education for their children and a wider range of job opportunities for the adults; in the 1950s, 14 more families moved into the neighborhood. Although many of these people did not remain in the area, at the time that Emma and John Martinez arrived in the early 1950s, the immediate neighborhood was home to around ten Latino families, four or five black families, and some Italians, as well as Anglos.[46]

The second- and third-generation Hispanics living quietly and respectably in this sub-community were closely knit, sharing a culture that combined features of the Mexican and the New Mexican/San Luis Valley backgrounds of their forebears. They were eager for their children to receive a good education, ideally completing high school and perhaps even going to college; they tried to increase the children's cultural and social acceptance into the surrounding Anglo community.[47] It was here that we encounter the first evidence of how some young people attempted to define their ethnic identity during the 1950s and early 1960s.

We know a good deal about the Water + Goss Streets area, its families and its culture. Some of its residents or former residents were interviewed in the late 1970s and in 2013, and the Boulder Hispanic Families project of 2012 gathered information and photos from about 40 families who had lived there at some time before 1955. One of the outcomes of the 2012 project was a detailed map of the neighborhood around 1955, prepared by Phil Hernandez. It used color coding to display Latino, African American, Italian, and Anglo households, with the names and addresses of all Latino families marked by number.[48] We must

---

[44] "Boulder's early black and Latino neighborhood."
[45] "Boulder Latino families."
[46] Martinez, Emma Gomez, interview, 2013.
[47] See Vol. I, Ch. 5C.

Illus. 2.3. Gilbert, Dolores, and Rudy Martinez in Boulder, 1948

remember, however, that the neighborhood was atypical in its economic stability, social cohesiveness, and access to education. The experiences of its residents were often quite different from those of Latinas/os living elsewhere in Boulder County.

Latinas/os who grew up in the Water + Goss Streets neighborhood described the positive interactions between residents, whether from similar or different backgrounds. They liked having other Latino families living nearby. When David Toledo's family moved to Boulder in 1943, the seven Mexican American families in the area already formed a community.[49] Roy Maestas spoke warmly about the 1940s and 1950s, when Mrs. Archuleta lived next door to them on Water Street and the Martinez and Bernal families were further down the street.[50] At the same time, although family-based sociability occurred mainly with people of their own ethnicity, diverse households met while shopping at the few small stores in the area or in giving assistance to neighbors who needed help. Their many children played together.[51] Virginia Madrigal Martinez

[48] "Map of central Boulder by ethnicity, 1955," and "Map of Boulder's Water + Goss Streets neighborhood by ethnicity, 1955."

[49] Toledo, David, interview, c. 1978.

[50] Maestas, Roy, interview, 1978. See also "House at 1718 Water Street, Boulder."

***Illus. 2.4.** The Tafoya family in front of Water Street home,
Boulder, 1956, with their car behind them*

described the African Americans who lived near her family as good
people who cut their grass regularly and kept their homes painted and
neat.[52] Although they went to a different church and had different social
customs, they were "quiet, caring, and cared about their neighbors."
Latinas/os who lived in other parts of Boulder spoke of feeling rather
isolated, not welcomed into that tightly-knit group of families.[53]

Although the friendship and cooperation that marked the Water +
Goss Streets community were described with real affection by former
residents, most Latino families moved to that neighborhood in part
because there was very little housing open to them anywhere else in
Boulder. This was to some extent a matter of the town's generally high
standard of living: relatively few low-cost rental units or small houses
existed in any area. Some realtors and homeowners during the later
1940s and 1950s probably made it difficult for Latinas/os to buy houses
in nicer "white" neighborhoods. But by 1960, when George Abila and his
wife moved to Boulder, George was not aware of any discrimination in
housing.[54] The realtor showed him houses in various parts of town, and

---

[51] For photos of children in that neighborhood, see Vol. I, Illus. 6.1, "Arroyo children,
    1942" (photo and text)," "Gilbert and Margie Espinoza at Central Park," "George Ara-
    gon with sons," and "Archuleta siblings."
[52] "Madrigal family of Boulder, biographies."
[53] E.g., Lehmann, Jessie Velez, interview, 1978, and Bernal, Dora, interview, 1978.

when he purchased one in an integrated neighborhood, people there treated him well.

The Water + Goss Streets community began to split up in the 1950s and 1960s. Small-scale urban renewal led to the tearing down of some of the older houses, replaced by modern apartment buildings. "Gentrification" contributed too, as young Anglo families started buying homes in the area and fixing them up. The growth of the University led students looking for inexpensive housing to rent some of the homes. Over time, some of the original Latino families decided to sell their homes and buy newer, larger, and more comfortable houses in other parts of Boulder or recently built subdivisions in Longmont, Lafayette, or Louisville.[55]

The interactive maps indicate that the small number of Latinas/os who lived in Boulder through the 1950s were quite dispersed. In 1936, when the Water + Goss Streets cluster was starting to emerge, there was a secondary concentration near the university and a smattering of households in other parts of town. Ten years later, the density of Latino families in Water + Goss Streets had increased. That neighborhood remained popular with some Latinas/os even in 1965 and 1975, now including students, but it was dwarfed by the greatly increased presence of Latinas/os elsewhere. A concentration of Latinas/os in the area east of 28th Street (U.S. 36) between Baseline Road and Colorado Avenue reflects the development of modestly priced rental housing there, including apartment complexes, used by University students and low-income families; another cluster is visible in the region of southeast Boulder between Moorhead and South Broadway, built after World War II primarily as "starter" homes for veterans.

Longmont apparently lacked a stable Hispanic neighborhood with a strong sense of community like those found in Lafayette and Boulder. During the 1920s and 1930s, some of the beet workers lived during the winter in the *colonia* built by the Great Western Sugar Company along the railroad tracks near its factory. This cluster of very basic housing was, however, far smaller than most of the other *colonias* built by the company, including the one in Greeley.[56] Dora Bernal and her husband did agricultural work on a different farm each summer between 1925 and 1936.[57] But they lived during the winters in Longmont's *colonia*,

---

[54] Abila, Mr. and Mrs. George, interview, 1978.

[55] See, e.g., Maestas, Roy, interview, 1978.

[56] For *colonias* more generally, see Hamilton, *Footprints in the Sugar*, pp. 281-286, and Lopez and Lopez, *White Gold Laborers*, esp. chs. 2 and 4-8.

rather than returning to the San Luis Valley, as Dora's parents had done. "If you put in an early application and were lucky, you could get a rent-free house of one room with a cement floor. Hardly a house. No electricity, no water inside." All the families shared an outdoor pump. In February or March, the beet farmers would come to the *colonia* to look for families willing to sign a contract for the coming season's work. The *colonia*, which also sponsored social events, had apparently closed down by around 1940.[58]

It is commonly believed by both Latinos and Anglos in Longmont that Latinas/os lived almost entirely east of Main Street and that segregated housing was enforced at least into the 1970s. The interactive maps, however, qualify that picture, especially for the first half of the twentieth century. (This is an instance in which quantified evidence calls into question people's subjective impressions.) Through 1946, these maps show some Hispanic families on the southern edge of town, extending from the railroad tracks (along 1st Avenue, close to the Kuner-Empson cannery and the turkey processing plant) up to about 3rd Avenue. Another cluster grew up in the blocks on either side of Martin Street between 3rd and 6th Avenues; a third group of families lived near Main Street between 9th and 11th Avenues, mainly on the west side of Main.

During the 1920s, 1930s, and early 1940s, the central figures in one neighborhood were J. H. and Sabina Cortez, who lived with their children and grandchildren along 3rd Avenue, near Martin and Atwood Streets. Described by his great-granddaughter as the closest thing Longmont had to a *patron*, "J. H. had no money, but he had charisma, wisdom, common sense, a wide network of friends and associates, and he was trusted and eminently respected by all."[59] On warm evenings, J. H. and Sabina

> could be seen relaxing on their front porch, J. H. in his overstuffed chair and Sabina in her rocker, both of them smoking their pipes. Passersby nodded and greetings were exchanged. With the distinguished manners that were then so prominent, people who wished to stop and visit asked politely for permission to approach, "*Con su*

[57] Bernal, Dora, interview, 1978.
[58] See Ch. 4B below.
[59] "Cortez, Jose Hilario ("J. H.") and Maria Sabina, biography" for this and below. J. H. was also active in politics, though behind the scenes: during meetings held in the parlor of their house, he educated Latinos about current issues and encouraged them to vote.

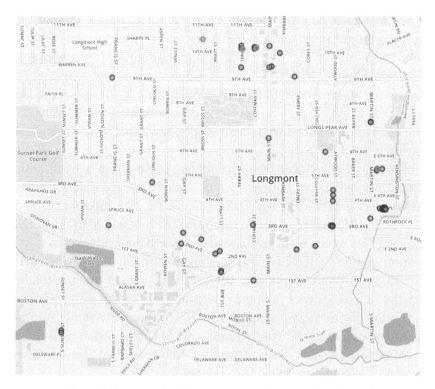

Illus. 2.5. *Screen shot of interactive map showing Latino-headed households in Longmont, 1946*

permission," and J. H. would, just as politely, extend an invitation, *"Pasa le."*

By 1956, however, Longmont's housing pattern was beginning to change. The northern cluster was less prominent, but many families still lived east-west along 3rd Avenue or between Collier and Lashley north of 3rd. The map for 1965 shows a greater density of Latino families on the east side of town: from Collier to Lashley, and from 3rd Avenue to Longs Peak. This distribution provides partial support for the idea that there was a de facto ghetto east of Main Street. But 1965 also saw a much larger total number of Latino families in Longmont, some of them living in scattered homes in western and northern parts of town that had previously housed only Anglos.

The increasing localization of Latino families in eastern Longmont in the 1950s and 1960s probably stemmed largely from the action of real estate agents. After the U.S. Supreme Court ruled discrimination

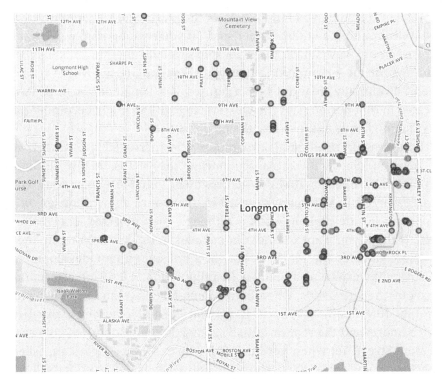

Illus. 2.6. *Screen shot of interactive map showing Latino-headed households in Longmont, 1965*

in housing illegal in 1948, realtors in many parts of the country began to promote de facto segregation by showing houses in certain neighborhoods only to whites and directing people of color to other areas. By 1975, however, Latino families were living all over the town, though the older housing clusters remained.

One factor in the breakdown of concentrated housing in Longmont was the increased prosperity, education, and assertiveness of some long-term families who insisted that realtors show them houses they liked and could afford, regardless of the neighborhood. The first little house that Hank and Esther Blazón (both from local families) bought after their marriage around 1960 was located east of Main Street.[60] But in the 1970s, they decided to upgrade, for Hank was then working at IBM and Esther had a good job too. The first two realtors they contacted only showed them houses on the east side of town, despite Esther's

[60] Blazón, Esther, interview, 2013.

statement that they wanted to look on the west side. Finally they went to a third realtor, to whom Esther said, "If you're not going to show me houses on the west side of town, let's not even do anything. It's just not working for me—I am asking that you show me houses where I want them." Eventually they did find a house near Longmont High School, located in that period near the western edge of the town, becoming the first Latino family to move into the neighborhood.

Pressure for residential integration was increased by the arrival of new middle class Latinas/os during the 1970s, many of them professionals hired by IBM.[61] When engineer Beto Moreno and his wife Marta wanted to buy a house in 1976, they were shown houses only on the east side of Longmont.[62] Although they objected, the realtor said, "I think you want to find a home over here," and eventually they acquiesced. Later the Morenos bought a house in a new development in the southwestern part of town. Discrimination in housing was falling apart by the late 1970s, when Emma Peña-McCleave and her husband, another IBM family, moved to Longmont.[63] The McCleaves wanted to buy a house, and the realtor initially showed them properties only east of Main Street. Yet when her husband, who is African American, asked specifically and forcefully to see some houses he had noticed for sale on the west side, the realtor agreed, and they ended up buying a home in what had formerly been an entirely Anglo neighborhood.

This chapter has demonstrated the gradual improvement of housing for many Latinas/os, though not for migrant workers. Over time, families who had previously lived on the edges of farms or in mining camps moved into towns, and those who could afford it were eager to buy their own homes. In each of the three towns, one or more low-income neighborhoods with many Latino residents emerged, though they included people from diverse backgrounds, unlike the heavily Latino *barrios* of some major cities. In Boulder, residents of the Water + Goss Streets area developed shared cultural patterns that incorporated elements from their Mexican and New Mexican backgrounds, and they

---

[61] See Vol. I, Ch. 6C.

[62] Moreno, Marta Valenzuela, interview, 2013. Beto remembered that African Americans hired by IBM did not want to live in Longmont at all, due to the residual influence of the Ku Klux Klan (Moreno, Heriberto ["Beto"], interview, 2013). For the Klan, see Vol. I, Ch. 4B.

[63] Conversation with Marjorie McIntosh, July 30, 2013.

promoted the education and social acculturation of their children. The interactive maps show that although Longmont is thought to have been ethnically segregated, there were several clusters of Latino households in different parts of the town in most decades. Only in the 1950s and 1960s do we see a higher concentration of Latino residents in an area east of Main Street, probably resulting from the activity of local realtors.

Chapter 3

Food, Health, and Medicine

The food Latinas/os ate—which often differed from that of Anglos—and the role it played within families were central components of many people's cultural identity. Cooking and eating meals together were part of the gatherings of relatives and friends.[1] Preparing traditional foods with family members for religious holidays remained one of the most enduring features of local Latino life right through the twentieth century, even among families that had adopted Anglo patterns in certain other respects. There were, however, differences in the types of food consumed depending upon the household's economic level and where they were living; as more women began to work for wages outside the home, ease of cooking might supplant a preference for traditional meals. Health care was closely related to cooking, as most medical assistance until the 1970s or 1980s was provided informally at home or within the neighborhood. Traditional remedies were based upon herbs grown and prepared generally by senior women. Only in the later 1970s did more than a few Latino women and an occasional man begin to enter the field of professionalized western health care.

A. Food

Cooking and serving food was almost always done by women. Daily meals were generally quite simple, with more involved items prepared for special occasions. The recipes for favorite dishes were rarely written down but were instead transmitted within families, as older women taught their daughters and granddaughters how to cook.[2] Normal meals were filling and nourishing but made from inexpensive and often homegrown ingredients. When Teresa Alvarez was living with her

[1] For food's role in social and religious occasions, see Chs. 4A and 5B-C below.
[2] See, e.g., Vol. I, Ch. 3D.

husband and eight daughters in mining camps or Lafayette during the 1920s and 1930s, she had to feed the family on very limited resources.[3] Any purchased food came from local stores, but they sometimes refused to give her credit until her husband's next pay. Every day she cooked beans and potatoes, she kept chickens for eggs and had a vegetable garden, and when she could, she bought milk for the children. Meat was a luxury. Patsy Cordova, when talking about her childhood in Longmont in the 1940s and 1950s, recalled, "Mine was a very loving home. . . . We ate beans and tortillas every day, and I didn't even know that we were poor because we were so rich in things more important than money."[4]

Many families grew their own vegetables. Even if they had ready access to a store, the food sold there was expensive, and the range of items might be limited. Cecelia Arguello said that her mother, who was raising a dozen children on her own in Longmont after her husband died in 1947, "had a natural green thumb. . . . She grew corn and other vegetables that would feed her family through summer and beyond, with what she canned."[5] Eleanor Montour, explaining that her parents used every inch of their back yard in Lafayette for growing vegetables in the 1950s, pointed out that Latino families from that period should get credit as early practitioners of organic gardening, since they did not use chemical fertilizers or pesticides.[6]

Although many women had to stick to basic cooking because they could not afford luxuries, homemakers among settled second- and third-generation families who had more economic leeway commonly prided themselves on special dishes. In the decades around 2000, younger relatives described with considerable nostalgia the meals formerly prepared by their stay-at-home mothers and grandmothers. Clofes Archuleta lived in the Water + Goss Streets neighborhood in Boulder. Her family thought that her red cooking bowl was magic, for it produced such wonderful food.

Virginia Madrigal Martinez said that her grandmother, Guadalupe Madrigal, another Boulder resident, "was one of the best cooks I have

---

[3] Alvarez, Teresa, interview, 1976.

[4] Cordova, Patsy, interview, c. 1987.

[5] "Arguello, Alfredo and Donaciana and family, biography." She also raised chickens for eggs and meat. The family got by thanks to government assistance for children.

[6] In a walking tour of Lafayette with Ana Gonzalez Dorta, a videographer, and Marjorie McIntosh, July 29, 2013; Ana used some of that footage and Eleanor's descriptions in her film, "Lafayette, film of places of historical importance," but not this bit.

Illus. 3.1. Clofes Archuleta and her homemaking skills

Clofes wore many hats as a wife, mother and homemaker. She was a master at handcrafts and sewing. She used an old foot pedal Singer sewing machine to make clothes for the children and embroidery helped her relax, as well as provide décor for the house. Her cooking was the best. The family believes her red bowl to be "magic" because her recipes can't be duplicated. She would make rice pudding, "migas" (bread pudding), tortillas, and homemade baked goods using the "magic" bowl. For the pantry she canned tomatoes, peaches, pears, and apples. She would create her own homemade remedies using medicinal herbs for headaches and upset stomachs.

ever known. Grams had a knack for cooking, making bread, soup with *albondegas, mole, tamales, enchiladas, buñuelos*, and making cheese. I was shown how to cut up a chicken in just a few minutes."[7] Virginia especially enjoyed helping her grandmother prepare *buñuelos*. The older woman would make a heavy dough, put a tea-towel on her knee, and stretch the dough across it until it was thin; she would then put pieces of the dough into peanut oil to fry. To enhance the treats, she put cinnamon or an almond-flavored syrup on top. But as time passed, especially as more women took paid employment outside the home, special foods were reserved for holidays and important family gatherings. Virginia said in 2012 that she still made *buñuelos*, but only once a year. Younger Latinas by the 1970s were starting to introduce easily prepared food from other cultures into their families' menus.

Food was an essential part of hospitality, even if it was simple. Linda Arroyo-Holmstrom, who grew up in the Water + Goss Streets area in the 1960s and early 1970s, said that food was part of the sociability whenever relatives or friends came over to her grandparents' house.[8] "Anybody could come in, drop in. . . . I don't know how they did it,

---

[7] "Madrigal family of Boulder, biographies."
[8] Arroyo-Holmstrom, Linda, interview, 2013, for this and below.

Illus. 3.2. *Miners at Leyden Mine, Lafayette, 1909?, with lunch buckets*

because grandma would start making tortillas—make a big bowl of masa tortillas—and she'd be rolling them, and that stack never grew. One person after another would be taking those tortillas, and so they were feeding everybody."

Coal miners had special food needs. They generally left home early in the morning after a large breakfast, carrying their lunch and water with them. Teresa Alvarez described what happened on winter mornings when her family was living in Boulder but her husband worked at a mine in Lafayette.[9] Teresa got up at 4:30 a.m. to "get breakfast for that man of mine." She made four to six small tortillas and fried "his chile con carne—pork, chili, and beans—and made him tacos" to eat with his coffee. For his lunch, she gave him bread, butter, and lunch meat.

As an older woman, Oli Duncan wrote that she had recently been stunned when she learned the reason for the peculiar design of her dad's and other miners' lunch buckets. The pail was cylindrical in shape, with a large bottom part to hold water and a top part for food.

> What I did not know was that the bucket was designed with its large reservoir for water in case there was a cave-in and the miner was stranded, needing that water while awaiting rescue. What I

[9] Alvarez, Teresa, interview, 1977.

also did not know was that, not just Dad, who I thought saved a bit of his lunch as a treat for his children, but miners in general did not eat all of their lunch, again in case of a cave-in; the half sandwich, or whatever, would help sustain them, along with the water, while awaiting rescue—assuming they were alive.[10]

Because Latino food was different from what most Anglos ate, it sometimes caused embarrassment or subjected children to ridicule, especially in the decades before Chicano pride. Patsy Cordova said that when her mom was young, "If anyone came unexpectedly at mealtime, the first thing my grandma would say was, 'Hide the tortillas'—especially if it was an Anglo at the door. . . . My mother still had the same reaction when I was growing up, . . . like it was a crime to have tortillas on your table."[11] A newspaper article about a reunion of old Boulder Latino families in 2003 commented, "Combining Mexican culture with the American way of life proved to be tricky in the 1950s."[12] Virginia Maestas was quoted as saying that "a stigma against all things un-American kept Hispanics from sharing their language, customs and food." She remembered her mother hiding tortillas, chile peppers and other traditional Mexican food items when non-Mexicans came into their home. Other people at the reunion recalled that Latino children "ate their lunches in the corner at school to hide their tacos or tortillas. They didn't want anyone to make fun of them for their different food, language, clothing or skin color."[13]

A few women were able to earn money by cooking. During the 1940s Teresa Alvarez paid for two of her daughters to attend Mount St. Gertrude Academy, a private boarding school in Boulder for wealthy Catholic girls, by working as a kitchen helper and cleaner.[14] She remembered peeling large buckets of potatoes, with a nun watching over her to be sure she did everything right. Margarita Solomon, who was born in Juarez, Mexico but crossed the border to El Paso to go to school, married her husband Manuel in 1978.[15] They moved to Longmont, where Manuel had relatives

---

[10] Duncan, "Dad," for this and below.

[11] Cordova, Patsy, interview, c. 1987.

[12] "Latino reunion" for this paragraph.

[13] Ibid. For children's embarrassment, see also Vol. I, Ch. 4B.

[14] Alvarez, Teresa, interview, 1977.

[15] Salomon, Margarita Macias, interview, 2009. Later, workers began to ask Margarita for help, "like buying money orders to send to Mexico, taking letters to the Post Office, or sometimes translating for them to the doctor." In 1986, after the Amnesty Law was passed, she and her husband, with the approval of the Tanakas, helped farm laborers to complete their applications for citizenship or legal residency and took them in groups into Denver to submit their papers.

who were working for Tanaka Farms.[16] When Manuel later became a foreman and their sons started working in the fields, Margarita made tortillas and burritos to sell to other Latino workers. "I would drive into the fields to deliver burritos and drinks to them. They were always very respectful to me." In Boulder, Señor Miguel's Restaurant was operated by Susie Gomez Chacon in the 1970s and later by her brother-in-law and sister, John and Emma Gomez Martinez.[17]

Mexican food gradually made its way into Anglo culture. Margaret Lindblom of the St. Vrain Historical Society recalled in 2006 that many years before there had been a tamale wagon on Main Street in Longmont, which she described as the town's first fast food place.[18] It was presumably frequented by busy Latinas/os, who lacked the time for traditional cooking, as well as some Anglos. Secundino Herrera of Longmont commented in the 1980s,

> There is more appreciation for Mexican food today than in the '50s. Before, they didn't think our food was suitable for human consumption. But now that they got used to it and found out the nutritional value and taste, they even recommend it. And the new cafes, even if they aren't Mexican they still list Mexican food to speculate with it, to capitalize on it.[19]

Food remained central to some Latino families into the twenty-first century. Arthur Perez was a chef at one of Boulder's leading (Anglo) restaurants when he was interviewed in 2013.[20] He reported that one of his grandmothers had been a chef, and his grandfather "was an executive chef back in the '50s and in the '60s, when Hispanics were not supposed to be in the power of management, but he was there (his ice sculptures were in magazines), and that's something that's been carried on in the family." When Arthur was asked about values important to his family when he was growing up in the 1980s and 1990s, he replied,

> I'd have to say the one big thing in our family was food. It's always been food. We'll have gatherings, and everybody has their own dish that they make, that is specific to their niche in the family,

---

[16] The Tanakas had come from Japan early in the century as beet workers but later became market gardeners. See Vol. I, Ch. 3A.

[17] Chacon, Susie, interview, 1977, and "Martinez, Emma Gomez, letter to her children."

[18] "A Rich Heritage," *Longmont Magazine, Daily Times-Call*, Aug. 12, 2006, p. 55.

[19] Herrera, Secundino, interview, c. 1987.

[20] Perez, Arthur, interview, 2013, for this and below.

cousins or whatever. And it's always great. . . . Menudo, tamales,
every holiday we're making tamales. We're not making one or two
dozen, we're making 45!

He felt that the food at gatherings helped to hold his extended family
together. Many Latino families now enjoyed going out to eat, especially
at Mexican restaurants, and busy women might buy dishes that took time
to prepare, like *posole* or *menudo*, rather than cooking them themselves.
But traditional foods eaten with relatives and friends retained their
cultural value even among families of mixed ethnicities. In 2012 Virginia
Madrigal Martinez still prepared *tamales* each Christmas with her
children, their spouses (who were from Ireland and England), and her
grandchildren.[21]

B. Health and Medicine

Prior to around 1950, and for some families long after that, going to
the doctor or a hospital when they were sick or had a minor injury was
not an option. Few people had the money or the time to go, professional
medical people rarely spoke Spanish, and women might be embarrassed
to describe their problems or reveal their bodies to a male doctor. Newly
arrived immigrants and migrant workers were especially unlikely to get
attention within the formal medical system.

In the traditional method of providing health care, senior women
were generally responsible for preparing remedies and tending those
who were ill within their families or communities. This is an area where
gender and generational factors were intertwined. Some specialists—
midwives, *curanderas*, or *curanderos*—served as healers for more than
just their own families and neighbors. With deep knowledge of plants
and how they could be used, and often with years of experience, they
treated people suffering from illnesses, injuries, and emotional problems.
They were thus practicing alternative medicine long before it became
fashionable. Midwives and *curanderas* commonly delivered babies too.
Highly respected within the local community, these Latina elders had
passed on their knowledge to selected younger women, ensuring the
continuity of assistance. Some of their remedies make excellent sense

---

[21] "Madrigal family of Boulder, biographies."

in light of modern scientific understanding, while other seem unlikely to have been effective in narrow medical terms but may well have been important in other ways.

Herbs formed the basis of most customary Latino remedies. George Abila, who grew up in Huerfano County in southern Colorado in the 1910s, listed some of the plants used there: *poleo* (pennyroyal, a medicinal herb in many cultures), *mariola* (sunflower), peppermint, oregano, and *chamiso* (saltbush, an evergreen shrub).[22] Roy Maestas said that when he was young, before and after his parents moved the family from northern New Mexico to southern Colorado about 1918, there were no diseases.[23] He could not remember getting seriously ill, which was lucky, since there were no doctors around anyway. Even after Roy's family came to Boulder County, stomach aches and other minor problems were cured with herbs: *chan* (*Hyptis suaveolens*, a relative of mint) and *Artemisia* (in the daisy family). *Aji* (in the pepper family) was good for headaches. Emerenciano Bernal and his wife said they never went to the doctor when they were younger.[24] For cuts, they used *osha* (a member of the parsley family that grows only in the Rocky Mountains) and for stomach problems, *mariola*. Later they were able to buy at Latino pharmacies some special medicines made from herbs: "Mexican oil," "Ahusari," "Sanadora," "Espiritos," and "Volcanic oil," the last used for broken wrists.

Sabina Cortez, who raised her own seven children and then seven grandchildren in Longmont, prepared a more elaborate set of medications. As a family member later recalled,

> Sabina was an encyclopedia of *remedios* for nearly every ailment. She was a great believer in the curative powers of camphor—as a tea or as an ingredient in any number of her medicinal concoctions. For example, she would add camphor to the potato and vinegar poultice applied on the forehead for headaches. She applied a mustard plaster for sore throats or chest colds. She browned flour in a cast-iron skillet and added cinnamon and water to boil up for a drink to cure diarrhea. Sabina was a big believer in enemas for fevers or constipation. She cooked onions with who knows what as an instant and effective cure for heartburn. She had a "magic plant" in her parlor, which was actually a giant aloe vera plant, good for cuts.[25]

[22] Abila, Mr. and Mrs. George, interview, 1978.
[23] Maestas, Roy, interview, 1978.
[24] Bernal, Mr. and Mrs. Emerenciano, interview, 1977.
[25] "Cortez, Jose Hilario ("J. H.") and Maria Sabina, biography."

Some problems, however, could not be cured. Children living in small, unheated houses with poor sanitation were particularly vulnerable. Maria Medina, born in New Mexico in 1891, had twelve children, three of whom died young: at 7 days, 16 days, and 5 years, all from undescribed illnesses.[26] Patrick Arroyo spoke of the dangers for children of pneumonia (one of his brothers died of that illness as an infant) and tuberculosis.[27] One of Dora Bernal's infant brothers died of diphtheria while the family was living in the San Luis Valley; her sister-in-law lost two brothers from that disease when they were children, and both of her parents died in the great influenza epidemic of 1918.[28]

Tuberculosis may have been a particular problem for young people in their teens. Of Teresa Alvarez's ten daughters, one died at birth, one at age 5 of leukemia, and one at 18 of tuberculosis.[29] Teresa believed that the older girl caught tuberculosis from Teresa's younger sister, after the family came to Boulder around 1940. She said in 1976 that she had not realized that her sister was contagious, "and maybe even if I would've known, I would've helped out my sister. My poor girl, she was the oldest one and old enough and wanted to help. Wanted to be kind and wanted to do things. . . . Sometimes we do the wrong things." Both Teresa's sister and daughter spent a little time in Boulder's sanitarium, but the family did not have enough money to keep them there, so they were tended at home for the several years before they died. In 1951, Johnny Rodriguez, another teen, went into the sanitarium.[30]

Several occupations were damaging to the health of Latino men. Coal miners were at risk from pneumonia and tuberculosis, and if they worked for a long period of time, they were likely to develop "Black Lung" disease. This illness stemmed from years of inhaling coal dust, which gradually built up in the lungs and damaged them, making breathing difficult and causing lack of energy and physical weakness. David Toledo, who started working as a miner in 1927, developed Black Lung disease some decades later; in 1966 he applied for compensation due to the illness, but after undergoing a health exam he had to wait three years before receiving a payment.[31] Mrs. Gomez of Erie, mother

[26] Medina, Maria, interview, c. 1978.
[27] Arroyo, Patrick, interview, 1989.
[28] Bernal, Dora, interview, 1978; Bernal, Mr. and Mrs. Emerenciano, interview, 1977.
[29] Alvarez, Teresa, interview, 1976.
[30] "Latino youth enters Boulder Sanitarium."
[31] Toledo, David, interview, c. 1978.

to Emma Martinez and Susie Chacon, told a high school class in 1967 that miners dreaded Black Lung, from which her husband was then suffering.[32] Teresa Alvarez, whose husband had Black Lung, said that eventually he became so weak he could not walk down the hall without holding on to the walls, and he was too uncomfortable to sleep.[33]

Some of the Latinos who worked with radioactive elements at the Rocky Flats Nuclear Weapons Plant later suffered from acute health problems. Al Cardenas was interviewed in 2004 when he was 70 years old and dying from berylliosis, a lung disease caused by exposure to beryllium.[34] He said that people were eager to get jobs at Rocky Flats when he started working there in the 1960s. No one described the risks of working with radioactive materials, and the workers would sometimes sit on piles of uranium ingots. He was very bitter that Rocky Flats had given its employees so little help when they became ill.

Concern with the lives of migrant workers on the part of established Latino families in the 1970s included their health.[35] A Migrant Health Clinic was operating in Longmont by 1977, while in Lafayette, Alicia Juarez Sanchez—a compassionate and forceful local woman—created the Clinica Campesina Family Health Services.[36] The Clinica was originally intended primarily for agricultural workers and current and former miners, but later it treated all low-income people. It provided care by Spanish-speaking professionals, helped people get prescription medications, and did health checks and gave immunizations to children so they could register for school and take part in sports. The Clinica also connected families with other forms of assistance, including the Community Action Program, the Employment Agency, Social Services, and Safe House. Located initially in a small house, it moved to a custom-designed modern building in which such groups could hold their meetings and activities. In recognition of Alicia Sanchez's contribution to the community, a new elementary school in a Lafayette neighborhood with many Latino children was named after her in 1986.

---

[32] Adelfang, ed, *Erie*, p. 41.

[33] Alvarez, Teresa, interview, 1976. He had died by the time she was interviewed in 1976, and she received a monthly benefits check from the mine.

[34] Cardenas, Alfonso, interview, 2004. For Rocky Flats, see Vol. I, Chs. 5A and 6C.

[35] See Vol. I, Ch. 6B.

[36] "Migrant Health Clinic gives guidance, care" and see "Five generations." Her face bore the marks of having had lupus as a child. The two clinic buildings and Sanchez Elementary School are shown in a film made in 2013, narrated by Alicia's daughter, Eleanor Montour: "Lafayette, film of places of historical importance."

Illus. 3.3. Alicia Juarez Sanchez and her award

Few Latinas in Boulder County held recognized health-related positions even within the traditional system. In northern New Mexico during the decades around 1900, being a midwife or *curandera* was a respected position for women, one that gave them considerable independence and authority. Emma Suazo Valdez said that her maternal grandmother, Antonia Chavez de Montoya, was a midwife in the area around Taos and Española from when she was in her 20s into her 90s.[37] "She would ride her mare as far as twenty miles to deliver babies," and she ushered into the world nine of Emma's thirteen siblings before the family moved to Longmont in 1942. Elvinia ("Bea") Martinez Borrego's grandmother was a midwife for many years, living until she was 105![38] None of the interviews done in the later 1970s and 2013 said that in Boulder County, designated Latinas had been responsible for giving health care and delivering babies. Further, as more people began to go to doctors or hospitals during the second half of the twentieth century, the role of older women as healers weakened. Informal midwives/*curanderas* nevertheless continued to provide assistance to some people.[39]

---

[37] Valdez, Emma Suazo, interview, c. 1987.

[38] "Borrego, Albert and Elvinia ("Bea") Martinez, biography."

[39] A community service worker reported in 2013 that new immigrants living in mobile home communities in Longmont knew who the local *curanderas* were; they went to them for medical advice and asked them to come when a woman was in labor.

The field of professionalized western medicine offered relatively little employment for local Latinas/os until the 1970s, mainly because most jobs required specialized education. No Latinas/os were listed in *Polk's City Directories* as working in health-related fields prior to 1940, with a gradually increasing number of women hired thereafter, mainly by hospitals.[40] In 1946, one woman was a nurse at the tuberculosis sanitarium in Boulder, and one Longmont woman was studying nursing.[41] Ten years later, Boulder was home to three nurses, and Longmont had one nurse and one female X-ray technician. Susie Espinoza was a Certified Nursing Assistant at Mesa Vista Sanitarium in Boulder, which cared for Navajo children from New Mexico and Arizona who had tuberculosis; she often brought some of them home with her for meals and to play with her own children.[42] The medical employment situation had changed little by 1965: two nurses and three nurse's aides in Boulder, and two nurses in Longmont.[43]

By 1975, however, we see a good deal of expansion, especially for women, thanks to the larger number of people completing high school and going on to higher education.[44] Lafayette had its first participant, a dietary aide who worked at Longmont United Hospital. Boulder now had three nurses and a medical aide, while Longmont had one nurse, three nurse's aides, a physician's assistant, a medical assistant, and a dietary aide, all women, plus one male X-ray technician. By the later 1980s, Gregory Jaramillo, who was later to be the director of the Salud Family Health Clinic in Longmont, was beginning his formal medical training, which included getting his M.D. at the University of Colorado Medical School and doing his residency at the Clinica Campesina in Lafayette.[45] In the next generation, many more Latinas/os were to move into health-related careers.

Although the particular kinds of food favored by Latinas/os could at times cause embarrassment, loyalty to traditional dishes remained strong across the generations. Even in the later twentieth century,

[40] See Vol. I, App. 3.2. For the *City Directories*, see Ch. 2, note 35 above.

[41] See "Occupations and Employers, Three Towns, 1946," "Occupations and Employers, Three Towns, 1955," and "Occupations and Employers, Three Towns, 1965" for this paragraph.

[42] "Asusena 'Susie' Espinoza."

[43] For successful efforts to become an LPN, see Mary Martinez, Ch. 6A below.

[44] "Occupations and Employers, Three Towns, 1975."

[45] Jaramillo, Gregory, interview, 2013.

preparing traditional foods continued to be a prized component of special gatherings and celebrations, including in families where women worked outside the home and normally had little time for elaborate cooking. The distinctive roles of senior women as sources of knowledge about recipes and remedies for traditional healing declined over time, but healthy and flavorful "Mexican" food and wise use of medicinal herbs may be seen as legacies to the wider community. The entry of Latinas/os into jobs within the western system of health care was delayed by requirements for formal training.

Chapter 4

Social Life, Entertainment, and Sports

Sociability among Boulder County's Latinas/os is related to the previous chapters, as it commonly involved family or neighborhood gatherings and included food. Early in the century, social interactions were largely confined to people living within walking distance of one's own home. For many farm families, the ability to make lasting friendships was curtailed by movement to a new job and therefore new housing every year.[1] But as more households acquired a car or truck, their ability to travel to meet with friends or join other social or recreational activities increased. Owning a vehicle continued to be a matter of pride, not just an economic necessity, as witnessed by many family photos.[2] By the middle of the century, young people were beginning to interact more often with non-Latinas/os than in the past, including around forms of entertainment and sports. Closer contact with Anglos heightened the need for an ethnic self-definition that validated one's ability to function well within the larger community.

A. Social Life

Many Latinas/os enjoyed an active social life. Until around 1950 and to some extent thereafter, it was almost entirely informal, concentrated within families and in some cases groups of neighbors or friends. In those earlier decades, social interactions varied a great deal depending upon where people were living. Urban residents had the most ample opportunities. In Boulder's Water + Goss Streets neighborhood, Latino

---

[1] See Vol. I, Ch. 3A-B.

[2] See Vol. I, Illus. 3.7, 3.8, and 3.9, Illus. 2.4 above, "Three boys in matching plaid jackets," "Two men standing in front of a car," "Six children in front of car," "Two toddlers on the bumper of a car," and "Young couple beside car."

households, some of them related, got together regularly to celebrate important events or just to enjoy each other's company. Virginia Maestas, who was born in 1935 and moved to Boulder around 1948, described what gatherings in that neighborhood had been like for young people.[3]

> It was kind of neat because there was no barrier between the young and the old. Most of our parents would be in the kitchen talking, eating, whatever. With the rest of the families, regardless of our ages, from young teenagers to the just over teenagers, all singing together and dancing together, laughing. Just having a good time. It was a real wholesome kind of entertainment.

For the Water + Goss Streets families, although many gatherings were associated with transition points in life or specifically religious events, a few other occasions called for a party too.[4] The holidays described by Marcella Diaz, who grew up in her grandparents' household in the 1940s and 1950s, were Easter (with no Easter eggs, just a family dinner), Thanksgiving (another family dinner), and Christmas (a big family assembly and meal).[5] "Christmas gifts were practically non-existent when we were children, though we did get a sock filled with mixed shelled nuts, an orange or apple, and one small gift that stuck out of the top of the sock. We had never received more, so we did not know enough to want more." In Virginia Madrigal Martinez's family, Easter was celebrated more vigorously in the late 1950s and 1960s. It was "a combination of egg hunts, lots of food, & lots of friends and relatives," plus homemade music.[6] Members of Boulder's Tafoya family received beautifully wrapped Christmas gifts in 1956.[7]

Some activities occurred outdoors. Patrick Arroyo remembered the corn and wienie roasts they had in Lafayette, where his father would tell stories.[8] They also played horseshoes, and he had informal boxing lessons. After his family moved to Boulder in 1944, he and some of his relatives went hiking around Flagstaff Mountain and the foothills, and his whole family had picnics at Chautauqua Park and went camping.[9]

---

[3] Maestas, Virginia, interview, 1978, for this and below.
[4] See Chs. 1B above and 5A below.
[5] "Martinez, Juan and Josephine; Marcella Diaz, biography." For New Mexican traditions at Easter, Christmas, and New Year's, see Cardenas, Lou, interview, at end.
[6] "Madrigal family of Boulder, biographies."
[7] "Tafoya family Christmas."
[8] Arroyo, Patrick, interview, 1989.
[9] Ibid. The photo below was taken by a German immigrant photographer whom Patrick's

Illus. 4.1. *The Arroyo family at Chautauqua Park, 1947*

Albert Borrego, who first trained horses for the Pace Ranch in Longmont and later worked as a miner, was described by his daughter and granddaughter as

> a great hunter and avid sportsman throughout his life. He passed on his hunting, fishing, and survival techniques, as well as his love of the outdoors and mountains, to his children and grandchildren during the many hunting, camping and fishing trips they took together. He loved to stream fish and hunted wild game up to the age of ninety-two.[10]

Juan Archuleta mixed business with pleasure by going fishing in the lakes and ponds around Boulder: during Lent his own family ate the fish, but normally he sold them to other people.[11]

The situation was different for early agricultural workers and their families. They generally lived on farms at some distance from other

parents had befriended: "Arroyo family at Chautauqua Park (text)."

[10] "Borrego, Albert and Elvinia ("Bea") Martinez, biography."

[11] "Archuleta family history," and see also "Man with large fish."

Latinas/os and had little time for socializing anyway. Roseann Chavez Ortega, born in 1942, lived as a child in the tenant house on Ralph Bixler's farm east of Boulder, where her father was employed. When asked in a later interview what her family did for entertainment or social life when she was a child, she said they did very little.[12] They did not have a television but listened to mystery programs and music on the radio. One of her mother's favorites was "Blue Heaven," which she sang as she worked around the house. Beyond that, they occasionally went to visit other families, mainly to the Garcias, who were only other Hispanics who lived close by. Migrant workers were even more isolated, finding it difficult to form ongoing friendships outside their own immediate families.

After the middle of the century, sociability increased among friends and members of extended families even if they did not live near each other. This change was due in part to more time off from work and improved communication and transportation. Hank Blazón, who grew up on his parents' farm in Mead, described their 4th of July tradition in the 1950s.

> My dad used to have his brothers and sisters over, and we'd barbeque a pig . . . or a goat or a lamb or something. Then after my dad stopped, ... we had it at my brother's who lives next door, and him and I used to roast a pig and we'd have people over and that probably went for ten years. We didn't do it last year but my niece has taken over, so she's starting the tradition to continue the barbeque on the Fourth of July. We've had up to 250 people here at one time.[13]

A few activities were carried out among wider circles of friends. Marta Moreno, who moved to Longmont in the mid-1970s, promoted some celebrations that had been common in El Paso, where she grew up, but were not regularly practiced here.[14] She thought these events would help to pull the Latino community together. She encouraged *quinceañeras* ("coming of age" parties for 15-year-old girls) and *posadas* (where groups of people walk to the houses of their neighbors and friends during the nine evenings before Christmas, asking to be allowed in, as were Mary and Joseph; when the "innkeepers" welcome them, they enter and all pray and then eat together). Dolores Silva and her

---

[12] Ortega, Roseann Chavez, interview, 1986.
[13] Blazón, William ("Hank"), interview, 2013.
[14] Moreno, Marta Valenzuela, interview, 2013.

husband Manuel had a lively social life in Lafayette. When interviewed in 2013, Dolores said that when they were younger, their friends "would have steak dinner dances with a Mexican band. That was our favorite thing to go to. We went to a lot of weddings. A lot of birthdays. A lot of *quinceañeras*. A lot of anniversary parties – because everybody more or less knew each other. So we would all invite each other to everything."[15]

Distinctively Mexican celebrations were rare in Boulder. Independence Day commemorated the beginning of Mexico's war against Spain on September 16, 1810. The day was still remembered by Virginia Madrigal Martinez's grandparents, who were 21 and 19 when they left Mexico and brought photos of the Independence festivities there, but they did not do anything to celebrate it in Boulder.[16] Marcella Diaz never heard of commemorations for the 16th of September when she was growing up.[17] The trans-national borderlands had evidently lost their meaning for those acculturated families: they did not share the strong expatriate Mexican nationalism found among some Latinas/os in California.[18] In Longmont, however, where many Latinas/os had come more recently from Mexico, hundreds of Spanish-speaking people enjoyed a two-day fiesta in September, 1935 to celebrate Mexican Independence, including patriotic speeches, entertainment, dancing, and a street parade.[19] The newspaper reported approvingly that "the entire fiesta was orderly and jovial." In the mid-1970s, Susie Chacon, the owner of Señor Miguel's Restaurant in Boulder, helped to create a Dieciséis Fiesta on a vacant lot.[20] But the turnout was disappointing, and it received no coverage in the press, so she was not sure it would become an annual tradition. A few Boulder families started celebrating Cinco de Mayo in the 1960s and 1970s, and there was somewhat greater enthusiasm for the event in Longmont, but prior to the late twentieth century, such fiestas did not assume the importance they had in parts of California.[21]

---

[15] Silva, Dolores, interview, 2013.
[16] "Madrigal family of Boulder, biographies."
[17] "Martinez, Juan and Josephine; Marcella Diaz, biography."
[18] Rosales, *¡Pobre Raza!*, p. 5.
[19] "Mexicans celebrate Independence Day."
[20] Chacon, Susie, interview, 1977.
[21] Hayes-Bautista, *El Cinco de Mayo*, pp. 177-190, and Alamillo, *Making Lemonade*, pp. 92-97.

Boulder Courthouse, 1940,
base of the WWI memorial
l to r: Arthur Archuleta, 16 yrs;
Victor Martinez, 16 yrs, friend;
Frank Archuleta, 14 yrs.

Illus. 4.2. Four friends in Lafayette, 1930s
(Sally Salazar Martinez, Pearl Lopez, Alvia
Abeyta, and Maggie Manzanares)

Illus. 4.3. Three friends in Boulder, 1940
(Arthur Archuleta, Victor Martinez,
and Frank Archuleta)

Illus. 4.4. Group of boys in Longmont, beside car

B. Entertainment and Recreation

Latinas/os took part in organized entertainment only occasionally. Virginia Maestas said that in Boulder during the late 1940s and 1950s,

> There was no place for the Chicanos, the Mexicanos, to get together, to have a good time, to have the cultural thing, music. We couldn't even get records in Boulder. If you wanted to buy a record and you were lucky, you might find one in Denver. There was one Mexican [radio] station that came into being around 1948-49.[22]

To see a Mexican movie, they had to go to Denver or Fort Lupton.[23] Aside from that, there were school dances, but Virginia did not like them, because the style of dancing was so different and much less fun. Virginia's comments draw our attention to the existence of a local cultural network that connected Boulder County to the large Hispanic population in Denver, 30 miles to the south, and to residents of the small town of Fort Lupton, 10 miles to the east, a center of sugar beet production.

Young people therefore organized their own activities or just hung out with friends.[24] In most settings, those friends were usually Latinas/os, but in Boulder's Water + Goss Streets neighborhood, boys had more diverse social contacts. John Martinez was friends with an African American boy from that area in the later 1930s; by the 1950s, most of Abe Maestas' high school friends were Anglos, young people he had known since their years together at Lincoln Elementary and Casey Junior High.[25] Integrated housing patterns thus promoted multi-ethnic, multi-racial activities.

Latino youngsters enjoyed many kinds of informal recreation. Patrick Arroyo, who was a teenager in the 1940s, described where they spent time: the soda shop next to the Isis Theater, the Alba Dairy ice cream shop, and Jones' and Potter's drugstores.[26] He and his friends went to the roller rink and swam at the indoor pool at the Hygienic Ice Plant, where

---

[22] Maestas, Virginia, interview, 1978.

[23] Virginia Maestas, conversation with Marjorie McIntosh, Nov. 24, 2013.

[24] See also "Jennie Razo (Romero) and Alicia Sanchez (Sanchez)," "Becky Ortega and friends," "Tina Perez and other teens playing poker," and "Four Suazo sisters as young women."

[25] Illus. 4.6 below; Maestas, Virginia, interview, 1978.

[26] Arroyo, Patrick, interview, 1989. He also recalled having to appear before Judge Bunzel, noted for his toughness, when a game of Ditch 'Em, an elaborate form of hide and seek, got a little out of hand!

Illus. 4.5. Patrick Arroyo and the "Boulder Belle," 1946

Patrick worked during high school. When he got older, he loved to drive his friends around in the family's 1929 Ford Model-A Roadster Ragtop. The Maestas children too went to the Hygienic Swimming Pool, located at 21st and Spruce, which cost only 10 cents; after swimming they would go across the street to the A & W place to get root beer and popcorn.[27] If Boulder Creek froze over in the winter, Abe and Bob Maestas played ice hockey, "using a tree branch for their stick and a smashed can for the puck." In the summer they fished in the creek and once went swimming in Baseline Lake. Lafayette offered more specifically Latino activities. When Eleanor Montour was in high school around 1960, she and her friends—most of whom had left school to start working—went "out in the community, going to dances, and listening to Mexican bands playing . . . and having that camaraderie and feeling of belonging."[28]

Few Latinas/os went regularly to the movies before the 1960s, in part because they were too expensive but also because the films were almost exclusively in English and local theaters were segregated. John Martinez described what happened when he went to the movies as a teen in the 1930s with an African American friend.[29] Longmont's movie theatre required Latinas/os to sit at the back or in the balcony. Alex Gonzales said that as soon as a Latino walked into a movie, the usher would tell

[27] "Maestas, Pedro (Roy), Ruby, and Abe, biography" for this and below. The A & W Root beer place is mentioned also in "Boulder, film of places of historical importance."

[28] Montour, Eleanor, interview, 2013.

[29] See also Martinez, Emma Gomez, interview, 2013.

SEGREGATION 1936

Emmett, the Geofos kid and I had gone to the movies downtown (Boulder).We had just sat down when an usher came up and told Emmett that Negroes couldn't sit on the main floor. He would have to sit in the balcony. We went with Emmett to watch the movie from the balcony. All of us were about twelve when this happened. I didn't realize until later that if I, as a Mexican American, had wanted to see a movie in Longmont; I would have had to sit in the balcony. The number of seats available to Mexicans was limited and Mexicans had to sit together in one area of the balcony.

Illus. 4.6. *"Segregation in Boulder, 1936," by John Martinez*

him which area to sit in.[30] Virginia Maestas remembered going to a movie in Longmont in 1950, when seating was still segregated.[31]

Because Latinas/os were excluded from some restaurants and bars until the mid-1950s, especially in Longmont and Louisville, men had to find other places to socialize.[32] Here as in other communities, pool halls were a place where Latinos could congregate. On the weekends after he finished hauling trash, Roy Maestas of Boulder would walk over to Bill's Billiards to have a drink and spend time with his friends, some of whom were Anglos.[33] Hank Blazón's father ran a pool hall in an upstairs room of the Dickens Opera House on Main Street in Longmont during the 1930s and early 1940s.[34] Although he was described in the 1936 *City Directory* as operating a billiards parlor, a more dignified term, he was nevertheless harassed by the police. In the 1940 U.S. Census, Daniel Martinez was listed as the manager of a pool hall in Lafayette. It served such a mixed clientele of miners that it was known locally as "the United Nations."[35] David Toledo, who worked mainly as a miner but also

---

[30] Gonzales, Alex, interview, c. 1987. Mexicans were likewise required to sit in separate sections of movie theaters in Corona, CA until after WW II (Alamilla, *Making Lemonade*, pp. 86-7).

[31] Conversation with Marjorie McIntosh, Nov. 24, 2013. The movie she saw was Mexican, which was unusual.

[32] Vol. I, Chs. 4B and 5C.

[33] "Maestas, Pedro (Roy), Ruby, and Abe, biography."

[34] Blazón, William ("Hank"), interview, 2013, and "Longmont, film of places of historical importance."

[35] Leigh Campbell-Hale, conversation with Marjorie McIntosh, March 25, 2013.

cut hair, opened a barbershop with pool tables in Frederick.[36] He sold sandwiches and coffee, and people played pool for money.

Music was an important element of Latino sociability and of a continued cultural identity. In Boulder during the 1930s and 1940s, E. E. Bernal "played the violin and guitar and would sing at family gatherings. Spontaneous dancing in the living room would occur when he began to play and sing a *corrido* or ballad in Spanish."[37] Virginia Madrigal Martinez said that at her family's Easter parties, "my grandfather would get out his mandolin, my dad, his guitar or bass, my uncle John, his violin, uncle Tony, his guitar, & uncle Frank would play his drums. And they would play all day long with aunts Mary Lou and Julie singing along."[38] Roy Maestas played the guitar and sang with family and friends; sometimes he brought other instrumentalists home to join the music, with his wife at the piano and his daughters singing.[39] Most of Roy's children also learned to play, some at school and others through private lessons. Abe played guitar, Phyllis, Alice, and Barbara played the violin, Martha played accordion, and Vivian played piano. Their parents' willingness to pay for music lessons and have them take part in school music suggests that they wanted the children to be comfortable with Anglo culture as well as maintaining Latino patterns.[40]

Some musicians performed for pay. Virginia Madrigal Martinez's grandfather and his sons had a band that travelled to other towns on the weekends to play for social events.[41] Mary Gonzales and her brother Alfonso used to sing—in Spanish—at weddings, baptisms, and other occasions in the 1950s.[42] Dolores Silva, who moved to Lafayette in the 1950s, sang at many events across the following decades, including weddings, funerals, *quinceañeras*, and anniversary parties.[43] People especially wanted her to sing familiar Spanish songs. As more bands with vocalists formed in the 1960s and 1970s, often to play at dances, some young Latinas joined Latinos in taking part.[44]

[36] Toledo, David, interview, c. 1978.
[37] "Bernal, E. E. and Eva, biography and photo."
[38] "Madrigal family of Boulder, biographies." See also "Juan Francisco Archuleta with guitar."
[39] "Maestas, Pedro (Roy), Ruby, and Abe, biography" for this and below.
[40] See Vol. I, Ch. 5C for identity formation among these young people.
[41] "Madrigal family of Boulder, biographies."
[42] Tafoya, Mary Gonzales, interview, 2009.
[43] Silva, Dolores, interview, 2013.
[44] "Two young men and a young woman playing guitars" and "Man playing guitar and woman playing accordion."

Illus. 4.7. *Ben Rodriguez at radio station KLMO, Longmont, 1952*

Many people loved "Spanish" or "Mexican" music. Ben Rodriguez, who later became the first Latino member of Longmont's City Council, hosted a popular Spanish-language radio program in the 1950s that played records of favorite music. Secundino Herrera, born in northern New Mexico but later a Longmont resident, said in 1987 that "Spanish-Mexican music is the most beautiful there is, and so is the culture."[45] Secundino and others in Longmont who enjoyed Spanish music were fortunate, for by around 1970, they were able to buy records at Casa Medina. Miguel Medina, a Puerto Rican who came to Colorado from Chicago, started with just a few LP records sent to him by a friend, but gradually he expanded his collection and his customers.[46] At least a few Latinas/os enjoyed classical European music as well. Ted Archuleta grew up in Longmont, graduated from high school in 1938, was a bomber pilot in World War II, and later obtained undergraduate and graduate degrees before becoming Dean of Business Services at a community college.[47] Even as a young person, Ted liked to listen to operas on the radio.

Dancing was popular among people of all ages.[48] When E. E. Bernal

[45] Herrera, Secundino, interview, c. 1987.
[46] Medina, Miguel, interview, 2013.
[47] "Archuleta, Ted, eulogy."
[48] See, e.g., "Dancing at a party" and "People dancing at a party."

Illus. 4.8. *Reina and Felix Gallegos dancing*

and his wife were working on beet farms around the county in the 1920s and early 1930s, they sometimes went dancing at a friend's house, joined by his parents and sister.[49] In Boulder, Juan and Clofes Archuleta danced "the silk scarf waltz" and polkas on family occasions.[50] A few dances were held in public places in the 1950s. John Chavez organized dances at the Elks' Club in Boulder on Saturdays, attended mainly by Latinas/os; Sacred Heart Church sometimes hosted dances, occasionally even hiring Latino musicians to play.[51]

Renting a space for private dances was another option. Roy Maestas said that although Boulder Latinas/os danced mainly in people's homes, once in a while someone would rent an upstairs hall on Pearl Street and hire a band.[52] Roy's daughter-in-law agreed. On special occasions, the teenagers—all of whom were working even if they were still in school— would get together and rent the W-O-W [or IOOF] Hall, upstairs on the corner of 11th and Pearl, for a fee of $5 or $6.[53] "For a particular birthday, or particular time of the year, we'd all pitch in and have the makings for

[49] Bernal, Mr. and Mrs. Emerenciano, interview, 1977.
[50] "Archuleta family history."
[51] Maestas, Roy, interview, 1978; Abila, Tom, interview, 1978.
[52] Maestas, Roy, interview, 1978, and "Maestas, Pedro (Roy), Ruby, and Abe, biography."
[53] Maestas, Virginia, interview, 1978.

a party. Bake our own cake, we'd make our own sandwiches, we'd have Kool-Aid. . . . So we teenagers (and we wouldn't exclude our parents, they were always welcome) . . . would have a really super good time."

Organized dances for Latinas/os were more common in Longmont. During the 1920s and 1930s, the *colonia* of minimal housing set up by the Great Western Sugar Company offered sociability for people who worked in the beet fields or the sugar factory, as well as for other Latinas/os living nearby. Benjamin and Adela Vigil lived across from the *colonia*. As a younger relative later recalled, "*La colonia* functioned as a social center for dances and other festivities for the local Hispanic community. When there were dances, young mothers took their children to Dela's house. There the mothers took turns tending the children so that they could also take turns enjoying the dance."[54] Patrick Arroyo, who spent his childhood in Lafayette and Boulder, remembered going to "jitney dances" in Longmont on Friday nights in the late 1940s and early 1950s.[55] Latinas/os would come from places all around, and he was introduced to his future wife there. Virginia Maestas likewise commented that dances in Longmont were where young people got to know Latinas/os from outside their own towns.[56] Some of those dances were held in the big hall above the Dickens Opera House on Main Street.

Less was said about Latino dances after around 1960. When Jessie Velez Lehmann moved to Boulder in 1962, she loved to dance but found she had to travel elsewhere to do so, as there were no public dances for Latinas/os in Boulder.[57] Candace Arroyo, a university student who was exploring what it meant to be a Chicana, was part of a *baile folklorico* dance group in 1977.[58] In the early twenty-first century, traditional dancing remained popular among older women. Mary Gonzales Tafoya, aged 74 in 2009, was part of a senior *folklorico* group called *Bailes de Mi Terra* that practiced twice each week for their performances at schools, senior centers, and other settings, dressed in elaborate costumes.[59] She was joined in that dance company by semi-retired Sister Rosa Suazo, also in her 70s.[60]

[54] "Cortez, Jose Hilario ("J. H.") and Maria Sabina, biography."
[55] Arroyo, Patrick, interview, 1989. At a jitney dance, you paid a small amount for entry and then a separate amount for each dance you wanted to join.
[56] Maestas, Virginia, interview, 2013. For below, see "Longmont, film of places of historical importance."
[57] Lehmann, Jessie Velez, interview, 1978.
[58] Arroyo, Candace, interview, 1977.
[59] Tafoya, Mary Gonzales, interview, 2009.
[60] "Sister Rosa Suazo (center) in Senior Folklorico Dance Group," and see Ch. 5A below.

A few short-lived Latino clubs provided social activities for some urban Latinas/os. Romolo Martinez was one of the organizers of the Spanish-American Club in Longmont. "The Club sponsored some fiestas in the '30s that were greatly enjoyed by citizens and visitors. Then at one fiesta some feisty young men from out of town got in a fight with the police and the celebrations were discontinued."[61] Virginia Madrigal Martinez's grandfather was president of his club in Boulder.[62] She said that whenever people needed help with problems, he would take them to Denver to the Mexican Consulate to get advice, but she did not describe what else the club did.

We have already seen the importance of veterans' organizations for former soldiers and their families, but the VFW played a wider role by renting out its facilities for private events.[63] When Dolores Silva was asked in 2013 where social events for Latinas/os in Lafayette had previously occurred, she responded:

> Most everything would take place there at the VFW. That's where Felicia had her *quinceañera*, and Chuck and Mandy were married there. They had steak dinner dances there. They had bingo there. Everything, everything you could think of—any kind of social thing—they had. You wanted to make money for a football team or a baseball team, they had everything done there at the VFW. The VFW was very, very good for all of us in Lafayette.[64]

C. Sports

Until around 1940, opportunities for participation in organized team sports were limited. Children and young people played informally with their friends and neighbors. Patrick Arroyo, born in 1930, remembered playing soccer and baseball first in Lafayette and then in Boulder after his family moved there in 1944.[65] Phil Hernandez and Tom Abila both mentioned a vacant lot—at the southwest corner of Water Street and 19th in Boulder—that was always filled with kids playing pick-up games

---

[61] *They Came to Stay*, p. 159. He was probably referring to an outdoor event called "Heroes of Mexico" held in Roosevelt Park in May, 1937, which ended in a fight; the police chief was injured when he tried to break it up ("Police chief attacked at Mexican celebration"). For the Spanish-American Club, see Vol. I, Ch. 5C.

[62] "Madrigal family of Boulder, biographies."

[63] See Vol. I, Ch. 5B for the G.I. Forum and the VFW.

[64] Silva, Dolores, interview, 2013.

[65] Arroyo, Patrick, interview, 1989.

of baseball or football.[66] The six Vigil children, who were living on the Lohr farm east of Boulder around 1950, used to play "Work-Up" baseball in the evenings, sometimes joined by their dad; when their friends the Griegos came for a visit, everyone played.[67]

In the 1940s, Latino young people—girls as well as boys—began to participate in sports at school, increasing their interactions with Anglo peers in non-academic settings. Doris Gonzales, born in 1928, recalled that she played field hockey, baseball, soccer, volleyball, and did track at school in Boulder—"everything they had then."[68] Tom Abila moved to Boulder in 1947, as he was entering Casey Junior High. Although he did not go on to senior high school, "I played baseball, I was on the wrestling team, started to play football but I couldn't do that because I was too light. I went out for track. I've always been athletic minded ever since I was young, and I've always competed. . . . That's where I really made my goal, in athletics."[69] Jim Hutchison, a scoutmaster in Lafayette for 30 years starting in 1955, encountered a similar attitude. Jim said that some of his Latino scouts were very smart but thought there was no future for them academically; athletics were the only way they could get ahead.[70]

Latino children involved in school sports were not always treated equally in those early years. Emma Gomez Martinez, who grew up in Erie, described many years later a painful episode in the mid-1940s:

> In 11th grade, I played volleyball. Our team won the championship. Lo and behold, there weren't enough letters for the girls, so mine was given to another girl. (I was the only Mexican on the team). My daughter wrote to Erie High School in 2012 and the principal sent me my overdue letter. What a sad experience for a 16-year-old girl. I had to beg my dad to let me play the following year.[71]

By the 1960s and 1970s, school sports were more genuinely integrated. In 1962, James Ortega of Boulder High School was the State Class A Wrestling Champion as well as a standout in football and an honors student; he planned to enter the University of Colorado that fall.[72] Gilbert Espinoza was a wrestling champion at Boulder High

---

[66] "Boulder, film of places of historical importance" and Abila, Tom, interview, 1978.
[67] Vigil, Jennie, and others, interview, 2001.
[68] Gonzales, Doris, interview, 2013.
[69] Abila, Tom, interview, 1978.
[70] Conversation with Marjorie McIntosh, Jan. 7, 2014.
[71] "Martinez, Emma Gomez, letter to her children."
[72] "Latino student graduates High School, 1962" and see "Latino students graduate High School, 1964, Pt. 2."

Illus. 4.9. Baseball team organized by St. John's Church, Longmont, 1946?

in 1964 and 1965; after serving in Vietnam, he received a wrestling scholarship to the University of Colorado.[73] Larry Rosales was one of Lafayette High School's three state wrestling champions in 1965.[74] Larry Zaragoza set a state record in track for Lafayette in 1967 and became a national champion in the 600-meter dash while at Adams State College in Alamosa; he then coached high school sports for 30 years.

Between the 1920s and the 1950s, some Latinos in eastern Boulder County played on competitive baseball teams. Most teams were segregated in those decades, with Latinos and African Americans excluded, so the "Sugar Beet League" was formed.[75] Its member teams were located in the towns of northeastern Colorado where many Latino

[73] "Gilbert Espinoza, State Champion, Wrestling Meet," "Gilbert Espinoza, State Wrestling Champion," "Gilbert Espinoza in Viet Nam," "Gilbert Espinoza's military service," and "Gilbert Espinoza, wrestler at University of Colorado."

[74] "Rosales, Larry and Linda, biography." The information below is from Phil Hernandez, email to Marjorie McIntosh, Jan. 13, 2015.

[75] "Sugar Beet Baseball Leagues." In this area, however, segregated baseball teams do not appear to have served as settings for emerging political activism as was the case in Corona, CA (Alamilla, *Making Lemonade*, pp. 128-129).

farm workers had settled, living often in *colonias*. The leading team in the region during the 1940s and 1950s was the Greeley Greys, whose members were heroes to the local Latino community.[76] Longmont was not part of the Sugar Beet League, but it had its own Latino teams, one of which was sponsored by St. John's Catholic Church and coached by priests. Later Casa Medina, the music store, and Joe Esquibel, pharmacy owner, sponsored teams.[77]

Segregation in baseball gradually broke down. Oli Duncan attributed the change to the increasing number of Latinas/os who went to high school in the later 1940s and 1950s.[78] When the coaches realized what good baseball players some of these boys were, they admitted them onto school teams. Once Anglos had become accustomed to integrated teams at school, they were more willing to let Latinos join adult leagues.

Baseball was popular as a spectator sport too. For some people, this interest began at an early age. Tom Abila talked about the influence of his grandfather, Abel Diagos, a former schoolteacher in Walsenburg who had moved to Boulder to be near his younger relatives.[79] One of the reasons Tom felt close to his granddad was that "he was a sports fan, especially baseball. He used to love his baseball. That's how come I got interested in sports, through him. He used to . . . explain it to me. The World Series and all that stuff. And that's where I started picking up sports, got enthused about sports."

At the level of professional athletics, Latinos in the Southwest were likely to participate only in boxing and baseball. John Ortega, born in 1895 and raised in Pueblo, became a prizefighter.[80] Competing under the name of "Johnny Kid Mex," he held the title of light-weight champion of the Rocky Mountain States for seven years during the late 1910s and early 1920s. But over time he did less boxing, taking work in the coal mines instead. In 1926, he, his wife Mary, and their five children moved to Lafayette, with no further mention of fighting. In the Longmont *City Directory* for 1936, Joseph M. Gomez's occupation is given as prize fighter.[81] He lived in a household headed by his parents, Andros and Minnie Gomez, at 1044 Bross Street, together with three other young male Gomezes who were beet workers. By 1940, however, Joseph was no

[76] Lopez and Lopez, *White Gold Laborers*, pp. 227-240.
[77] "Casa Medina's softball team" and "Joe Esquibel in 1989."
[78] Conversation with Marjorie McIntosh, April 12, 2013.
[79] Abila, Tom, interview, 1978.
[80] "Ortega, John, family of, biography" for this paragraph.
[81] "Occupations and Employers, Three Towns, 1936."

Illus. 4.10. *John Ortega as boxer "Kid Mex"*
in 1919

longer living in Longmont, and we do not know what his later history was.

Professional baseball players were likewise rarely mentioned. Dolores Silva said that when her mother came to Denver from Taos, New Mexico as a young woman in the 1920s, she met Dolores's father, a professional baseball player. After he stopped playing, he became a coal miner.[82] Miguel Medina had a different connection with the pros near the end of the century. In 1991 he met someone who played for the Denver Zephyrs, a minor league team, and through him got to know the Spanish-speaking players.[83] When the men moved into the major league, Miguel became the translator for Latinos like Vinny Castilla, Armando Renoso, and Andres Galarraga when they were interviewed or needed something in writing. He also worked with young players who were homesick and unhappy, encouraging them to stick with it: "This could be your future, and you got to, you have to do it . . . for you and for your family."

Social life and entertainment among Boulder County's Latinas/os moved from being almost entirely home- or neighborhood-based early

---

[82] Silva, Dolores, interview, 2013.
[83] Medina, Miguel, interview, 2013.

in the century to becoming part of somewhat wider cultural circles. Music and dancing were key ingredients of social occasions, in whatever setting, but until the later 1950s and 1960s Latinas/os generally had to take seats in less desirable sections of movie theaters and were excluded from many bars and restaurants. School sports were gradually integrated, but at a professional level, Latinos were confined to boxing or segregated baseball teams until the second half of the century. Limited participation in Anglo-dominated cultural and athletic events contributed to the ongoing role of the family as a focus of Latino social life.

Chapter 5

Religion

Since the beginning of the twentieth century, most Latinas/os in Boulder County have been Roman Catholics. Religion was generally very important to them, as individuals and as families. Religious rituals marked the key stages of life, and certain Catholic beliefs and practices remained part of many people's cultural identification even if they were not regular attenders at church. There were, however, marked changes across the span between 1900 and 1980. Prior to the mid-century, Hispanics were rarely involved in a parish community. Few lived within walking distance of a church, and even if they were able to attend Mass, they were not welcomed by the priests or other parishioners. Religious practice was therefore centered within the home, led often by a senior woman. As in other aspects of Latino family life, gendered and generational factors were significant. The 1960s and 1970s saw greater social and religious inclusion of Latinas/os within the church but also dissatisfaction among some local people with aspects of Catholic beliefs and traditions.

A. Latinas/os and the Local Catholic Churches Prior to the 1940s

Each of our three towns had a Catholic Church by 1910, built by Anglo members of the community. Boulder's Sacred Heart of Jesus was located in the downtown area, near the early Protestant churches and within walking distance of the Water + Goss Streets neighborhood.[1] The church of St. John the Baptist in Longmont was located one block east of Main Street, accessible to Anglo Catholics but convenient for Latinas/os

---

[1] See "Boulder Public Library and Sacred Heart of Jesus Church" for the church in 1931; for the church and school in 2013, see "Boulder, film of places of historical importance."

Illus. 5.1. *Bernal children's First Communion, 1951*

as well.[2] In Lafayette, the first Catholic church (St. Idas's) was erected in 1907, when the community was little more than a mining camp.[3] St. Ida's was later replaced by a small and then a large and architecturally modern Church of the Immaculate Conception.

Latinas/os who lived in urban areas commonly wanted to mark important life transitions with a religious ceremony, if they could afford the cost. In addition to baptisms, weddings, and funerals, which we have already discussed, the church provided religious education in preparation for First Communion and confirmation.[4] Children went to catechism and received their First Communion at the hands of their parish priest around the age of 6-7; at age 13-14, after more catechism, they were confirmed, this time by the bishop. Photos were often taken— and treasured within families—of children at those occasions.[5] A

[2] "St. John's Catholic church and parsonage," "Sanctuary, St. John's Catholic Church," and "Longmont, film of places of historical importance."

[3] *Lafayette, Colorado*, T103. For a video from 2013 that shows both of these churches and talks about their practices, see "Lafayette, film of places of historical importance."

[4] See Ch. 1B above.

[5] See "Becky Archuleta's First Communion remembrance," "First Communion, Josephine and Esther Arroyo" (photo and text), "Eddie Quintana's First Communion," "Rhonda

Illus. 5.2. *Sister Rosa Suazo with children at their Confirmation in Longmont*

celebration was then held at home. Yet interview material suggests that prior to the 1940s, some—perhaps many—families did not attend Mass regularly or feel a strong connection with any parish church. Especially for people living in rural areas and those who spoke little English, home was the center of prayer and even of religious instruction.

Detachment from the formal structure of the Catholic Church stemmed from multiple factors. Several related to the nature and location of people's employment. Agricultural laborers and miners commonly worked 6-7 days per week, with little if any time off to attend religious services. Most field workers lived on scattered farms, located at some distance from urban churches. If people did not have access to a car or truck, they had no way to get to Mass. The challenges were even greater for migrant workers, who were unable to form an attachment to any particular church. Miners living in dispersed camps likewise had no religious facilities nearby. Dora Bernal, born in 1911, said that as a child living in the San Luis Valley, she walked to church with her parents.[6] But

Gonzales' and another girl's First Communion," and "Brenda Romero at her First Communion."

[6] Bernal, Dora, interview, 1978.

when she and her husband began working on farms in Boulder County, they never attended Mass because they did not get Sundays off and there were no churches near them. After they moved into Boulder, they occasionally went to baptisms but did not attend church otherwise.

Limited Latino participation in local churches was due also to the negative attitudes of many of the Anglo priests and lay people who ran the parishes. Latinas/os were not greeted warmly at Catholic services, and seating was commonly segregated. Alex Gonzales of Longmont remembered with some bitterness that the church "didn't let us sit where there were books or missals. The priest would tell us to move."[7] The church in Lafayette was an important part of Eleanor Montour's childhood during the 1940s and 1950s.[8] Her Spanish-speaking grandparents, who could not read or write, were able to understand some of the Mass (which was in Latin until the mid-1960s), and her grandmother went to St. Ida's every morning. But Latinas/os had to sit very quietly at the back. Later, after the parish moved to Immaculate Conception, there was more mixing in services, with Latinas/os and Anglos sometimes sitting next to each other.

Nowhere in the county were there any Spanish-speaking priests or Spanish-language services until at least the 1970s. Latinas/os who were not fluent in English were therefore unable to go to confession and did not know what was being said during the sermon. Some Latino families in Boulder's Water + Goss Streets neighborhood attended Sacred Heart Church each week, but nearly all of them spoke English. The absence of Spanish priests and services was not a necessary feature of Catholic churches in the Southwest. Some people who had grown up in northern New Mexico or southern Colorado remembered that when they were children, Spanish-speaking priests staffed their churches and conducted services in Spanish.[9] Parishes in Huerfano County held Hispanic festivals, such as a three-day celebration of the Day of Santiago and the Day of Santa Ana.

Latinas/os cared about attending services in their own language. Mrs. E. E. Bernal was an elderly woman when interviewed in 1977. Still more comfortable speaking Spanish than English, she said that while she and her husband were seasonal beet workers in northeastern Colorado from

[7] Gonzales, Alex, interview, c. 1987.
[8] "Lafayette, film of places of historical importance."
[9] E.g., Abila, Mr. and Mrs. George, interview, 1978.

Illus. 5.3. *Secundino Herrera and Father James, Longmont*

1919 to 1934, she made her children go to church if one was available.[10] When the family settled in Boulder, there was no Spanish-speaking priest in Sacred Heart parish, and no visiting priests came from outside. She and her husband therefore made the trip "all the way to Denver" every Sunday to hear Mass at a church with a Mexican priest. Here is another connection between Denver and Boulder County.

An alternative form of Catholicism for a few Latino men was participation in the confraternity movement known as the *Penitentes*. Throughout northern New Mexico and southern Colorado during the nineteenth and early twentieth centuries, groups of *Penitentes* brothers met in special religious buildings, called *morados*, for worship and to carry out rituals not part of typical Catholic practice, including flagellation. J. H. Cortez was a member of a *Penitentes* group whose *morado* was in Fort Lupton.[11] (A local religious network evidently operated for alternative as well as conventional Catholicism.) As Cortez's great-granddaughter later explained, Cortez attended

[10] Bernal, Mr. and Mrs. Emerenciano, interview, 1977.
[11] "Cortez, Jose Hilario ("J. H.") and Maria Sabina, biography" for this and below.

Illus. 5.4. Suazo family in a beet field, early 1940s

the meetings and services with his friend, Onofre Romero, and others. The *Penitente* brotherhood had been driven underground by the Roman Catholic Church, which had been dismayed by its extreme religious rites. The *Penitentes* have since reclaimed their legitimacy and operate freely in New Mexico and, presumably, elsewhere. Apparently they have tempered their religious zeal.

Both Boulder and Longmont had Catholic schools, which offered some benefits to adults as well as carrying out their educational mission.[12] Teresa Alvarez remembered that when she moved to Boulder in the 1940s, mothers used to walk their younger children to Sacred Heart School and got to know other families that way.[13] Secundino Herrera worked for St. John's School in Longmont for 13 years, under the supervision of Father James and Father Martin.[14] He emphasized that although he learned a lot on the job, he also "contributed so much that it's hard to mention everything I did, along with other people." He saw their work as part of the unrecognized contribution of Mexican people to the community.

Probably as the result of the Catholic Church's unwillingness to incorporate Latinas/os fully into its activities, very few local people

[12] For Catholic schools, see Ch. 6A-B below.
[13] Alvarez, Teresa, interview, 1977.
[14] Herrera, Secundino, interview, c. 1987.

Illus. 5.5. *Sister Rosa Suazo when she took her final vows, 1953*

became priests, monks, or nuns. That pattern differs from the experience of certain other Catholic immigrant groups, like the Irish, for whom going into holy orders was a highly respected and readily available option. Apart from Sister Maria Regina Rodriguez, born in 1927 to a Lafayette family, the only local person encountered in this study who entered the church was Sister Rosa Suazo.[15] Born in 1933, the future Sister Rosa was one of 14 children of Daniel and Santos Suazo, who moved with their family to the Longmont area from New Mexico around 1940.[16] The father and older children worked at least part-time in the beet fields.[17] Sister Rosa attended St. John's School through eighth grade, where she greatly admired the Franciscan nuns who taught there. In 1950, at age 17, she entered the convent of the Sisters of St. Francis of Assisi in Milwaukee.[18] After serving her order there for 23 years, she returned to Longmont, where she worked primarily with immigrant families until her retirement in 1996. Even then she remained active. Sister Rosa was a

---

[15] "Sister Maria Regina Rodriguez." For Sister Carmen in Lafayette, see Vol. I, Ch. 6B.

[16] "The Little Rose" [Sister Rosa Suazo], a biographical newspaper article written when she retired.

[17] For photos of the Suazo family, stretching from the 1920s to the 1950s, see Vol. I, Illus. 5.1, and "Daniel and Santos Suazo," "Portrait of the Suazo children," "Suazo family in front of Lloyd Dicken's house," and "Suazo family," 1950-60; "Suazo family house" shows where they later lived.

[18] A later picture is "Sister Rosa Suazo (in white, on right)."

respected, even beloved, member of Longmont's Latino community, but she apparently did not inspire others to take holy orders.

B. Traditional Religious Practices at Home

Until at least the mid-twentieth century, many religious practices among Boulder County Latinas/os were carried out at home, whether they attended organized church services or not. The key figure was usually the senior woman of the family. When Teresa Alvarez, born in 1897, was a child, she lived in various places in Boulder County, with her parents until their death and then with foster parents.[19] When her father was working in the beet fields, the family lived on those farms; when he was employed in the coal mines, they lived in a camp next to the mine. In neither setting did they ever go to church, because they had no way to travel to a town. But, Teresa reported, "My mother was a Catholic; my foster mother was a Catholic. They had prayer books and they'd teach us catechism and all that at home. They told us things about the Lord, . . . but we never went to Mass."

The descriptions given by the children and grandchildren of these women make their domestic religious practices come alive. Marcella Diaz said that her grandparents, Juan and Josephine Martinez, were "Catholic but not involved in the church."[20] When they came to Boulder, they sent the children to church on Sundays but did not attend Mass themselves. Religious activity happened mainly within the family. When Marcella was young, in the 1940s and 1950s, "altars made to . . . Jesus, Mary, and other saints, and pictures of other saints and candles were common at home." Prayer was part of her grandmother's way of life. When she said, "'Let's go pray,' we knew we were in for a long period of kneeling, praying the rosary (*El Padre Nuestro y Santa Maria*) followed with a new novena every tenth day, or other prayer petitions, until she had her fill. Lenten season was an everyday prayer time for us, or anyone who intentionally wanted to join the family in Spanish prayer, and whoever happened to knock on our door during prayer time."[21]

[19] Alvarez, Teresa, interview, 1976.

[20] "Martinez, Juan and Josephine; Marcella Diaz, biography," for this paragraph.

[21] Gregoria Martinez was likewise the center of her family's religious life. "She would gather her female children and all grandchildren to pray the rosary every Wednesday and pray the Stations of the Cross on Friday during Lent" ("Martinez, Canuto and Gregoria, biography").

Sabina Maes Cortez, who lived in Longmont, maintained an altar in her house in the 1920s and 1930s. She felt greatly honored when she was allowed to host the "Traveling Virgin" from St. John's church "as the Virgin made her rounds throughout the parish."[22] She had various secondary religious practices too. "To keep evil out of the house, Sabina hung crosses over all of her doorways, especially over the front door. When there were bad storms, she would make the sign of the cross with salt, and then make the sign of the cross with a knife, outside, in the elements, to 'cut the storm.'" Sabina's religious piety led to high expectations for her children, grandchildren, and great-grandchildren: "Good behavior was never enough; she aimed for perfection, based on a very strict brand of Catholicism and imposed through her own iron will. If she thought they needed it, she did not hesitate to thrash a child with her cane—anybody's child who was misbehaving and within her reach."

Roseann Chavez Ortega, who was born in 1942 and grew up on farms in eastern Boulder County, said that although her family rarely went to church, her grandmother was religious.[23] "She had a little altar in her house. Whatever house she moved to, she made this little altar in the corner. It was usually the bedroom. She'd have curtains hanging in the corner. She'd have her saint there and her candle." Her grandmother believed in witches and witchcraft. "I don't think she practiced it but she was 'wise' to it. She knew about it. Always cautioning me, my mother, about being careful about meeting certain people. You could tell they were witches because of certain things." Roseann said that such talk "scared the h--- out of me!" Only one person interviewed in 2013—an elderly woman—referred to witches: they came up when she was describing a frightening person who had been on a long bus trip she once took.[24]

Cecelia Arguello wrote about the religious customs of her widowed mother, Donaciana, who was living in a small house in Longmont with her large family in the 1940s and 1950s.[25] Donaciana had an altar (really a dresser) that held her statues and religious items. "Once the hollyhocks bloomed in the spring, we younger kids helped our mother every day to cut the flowers and bring them inside to adorn the edges of the 'altar' . . . . To this day when I smell the hollyhocks in my own

[22] "Cortez, Jose Hilario ("J. H.") and Maria Sabina, biography," for this paragraph.

[23] Ortega, Roseann Chavez, interview, 1986.

[24] Gonzales, Doris, interview, 2013.

[25] "Arguello, Alfredo and Donaciana and family, biography."

yard, I am transported back to those days of my childhood." Although Donaciana made her children go to Friday night novenas and Sunday Mass at church, she had additional activities at home.

> Faith played a big part in my mother's raising her twelve children. . . . Christmas Eve we always made tamales and, while they were cooking, we would pray the rosary. After the rosary was prayed, Mother would pass around the ceramic Christ Child to receive a kiss from each one in attendance. Then she would lay the Child in the manger. (Until then the Child had been sitting up in a little chair that my mother had made.) This signified that the Christ Child was born, as by then it was a few minutes after midnight and Christmas day. Then we would enjoy the tamales.[26]

Some people prayed especially to a favorite saint or aspect of Christ or Mary. Oli Duncan's Grandma Nina "prayed her sons home" when three of them were in infantry divisions overseas during World War II. As Oli described,

> She performed an ancient ritual in their behalf. She collected all the religious statues and pictures (*santos*) in the house and placed them in a drawer where they would stay until her sons came home. During that time, no one in the household prayed for another thing. The *santos* were busy watching over the young soldiers. And all three of them came home.[27]

When Lou Cardenas's son was in the military in Vietnam, "I used to pray and pray that everything was all right. My saint is *el Santo Niño* [the Holy Child], and I used to pray to him and light candles and everything to keep my son safe. I guess all my prayers were answered. He came home all right."[28]

C. Involvement with the Catholic Church after the 1940s

From around 1950 onward, Boulder County's Catholic churches gradually became more hospitable to Latinas/os, reducing the importance of older women as organizers of home-based worship. As urban parishes started to introduce social activities, especially for young people,

---

[26] Ibid.
[27] "Olivas, Ralph and Rose, biographical account."
[28] Cardenas, Lou, interview, c. 1987.

Latinas/os were allowed to join. Tom Abila, who moved to Boulder as a teenager in 1947, remembered playing bingo and going to dances at Sacred Heart Church.[29] By 1963, that church had become more inclusive, with John S. Chavez, Jr. serving on its parish council, as a Eucharistic minister, and as an usher.[30] In Longmont, St. John's Church organized a baseball team for young Latinos in the mid-1940s.[31]

The late 1960s and 1970s saw some dissatisfaction with traditional Catholic beliefs and/or practices, especially on the part of Latinas/os whose families had lived in the U.S. for several generations. (New immigrants were generally more respectful of the official church.) A new assertiveness among lay people concerning the clergy and structure of the church was facilitated by the reform measures instituted in the wake of the Second Vatican Council, opened by Pope John XXIII in 1962. In Boulder, Latinas/os who were unhappy with the conservative theological stance of Sacred Heart of Jesus and its resistance to offering services in Spanish could move to St. Thomas Aquinas, the more liberal chapel that served the university and participated in community projects.[32] Susie Chacon, a local businesswoman, said in 1977 that she was not a regular churchgoer, but when she did attend, she went to St. Thomas Aquinas, not Sacred Heart, in part because the university parish had a Spanish priest.[33] In Lafayette, Sister Carmen's work with needy families and migrant workers during the 1970s led the Catholic parish to become more fully involved with the Latino community.[34]

A significant change beginning in the 1970s was the introduction of Spanish-speaking priests and Spanish-language services, including the Mass itself. This shift resulted largely from pressure by Latino members of the congregation, thus forming part of the wider movement of Chicano activism.[35] Marta Moreno, who grew up in a Latino community in El Paso, was heavily influenced by the nuns there.[36] When she moved to Longmont in 1974, she was shocked to find there were no services in Spanish at St. John's Church. So she prepared and circulated a petition

---

[29] Abila, Tom, interview, 1978.
[30] "John S. Chavez Jr. and Knights of Columbus."
[31] See Illus. 4.9 above.
[32] See, e.g., its role in creating Alvarado Village and its Social Action Fund, Vol. I, Chs. 6C and 7A.
[33] Chacon, Susie, interview, 1977.
[34] See Vol. I, Ch. 6B.
[35] See Vol. I, Ch. 7A
[36] Moreno, Marta Valenzuela, interview, 2013.

proving that 250 Spanish-speaking families in the parish wanted to hear the Mass in their own language. By 1977, St. John's was offering a Spanish Mass on the third Sunday of each month, conducted by visitors.[37] Somewhat later the parish hired its own Spanish-speaking priest. The Morenos also helped to start a Hispanic choir at the church, which gave them and other Latinas/os a chance to sing religious music they loved, in Spanish.[38]

Such measures had an impact on Latino participation in services and parish activities. Secundino Herrera commented in 1987 that St. John's church had started having a weekly Spanish service. This was good, "because people will now understand what's being preached and they'll go and listen and concentrate on what's being said."[39] Reina Gallegos, born in 1937, said in an interview 50 years later, "I have always been a very devoted Catholic whether I go to church or I don't."[40] As a child, her family prayed at home, and when she moved to Longmont around 1975, she could not find a church where she was welcomed. For the past few years, however, she had felt much more at home at St. John's: "the best thing that's happened to the church is Father Padilla being there." Reina talked also about the beautiful shrine that had recently been erected at the church: "Our Lady of Guadalupe, the *virgin madre de los mejicanos*, . . . is to me a very beautiful thing. I understand that the shrine was put in by *la gente mejicanos*." When the *Coro San Juan* was set up at the church, Reina joined it. "I love to sing. And I especially love to sing to my God."

A few people were upset with the Church on theological grounds. Virginia Maestas described the conversations about religion she had had with her grandmother in a rural area of the San Luis Valley, as she kept the older woman company during walks to meetings or services at church.[41] Virginia believed that those discussions had led her to think more independently about religious issues. When she and her husband moved to Boulder in 1969, they joined a discussion group at Sacred Heart Church to explore such elements of faith as the "Our Father" prayer. But when Virginia brought up questions about what the doctrines really meant, and what relevance they had for people today, the priest running the group criticized her. At that point, she shifted to St. Thomas Aquinas,

---

[37] "Longmont, film of places of historical importance."
[38] Moreno, Heriberto ("Beto"), interview, 2013.
[39] Herrera, Secundino, interview, c. 1987.
[40] Gallegos, Reina, interview, c. 1987, for this paragraph.
[41] Maestas, Virginia, interview, 1978.

which she described as a more diverse community, with people from all over the world and a more open-minded stance about faith.

Similar experiences led Yolanda Arredondo to stop attending church entirely. Yolanda—the director of Boulder's Safehouse for abused women—said in 2003, "I was raised Catholic, so I'm baptized and communioned and confirmed and all that stuff. I don't practice Catholicism any more. I don't actually practice any religion."[42] When she was young, her parents expected her to go to church every Wednesday and Sunday. Even as a child, however, she was having difficulty accepting official doctrine. When she went to confirmation class, she would ask the priest questions but never get answers. "They'd be like, 'Shut up, Yolanda. Don't ask. Just learn your verses.'" One of the issues she raised was why the Church had used "the Bible and God to justify having slaves. That to me would be the ultimate sin.... What you're doing is imprisoning another human being. That's evil. In my mind that's absolutely evil."

When Yolanda went to college, she was free to analyze the Catholic Church and its beliefs on her own. "What I came up with was that the church I grew up in was very patriarchal. Finances were very important to the church." She disagreed with some of the policies of the church too. Why, for example, did it consider her mother a sinner and refuse to allow her to re-marry with its blessing because she had divorced her husband; whereas her mom's first husband, who had had an ongoing affair with another woman during their marriage, was allowed to remain a Catholic in good standing? Noting that her parents were disappointed with her for not continuing to practice religion, Yolanda concluded: "I do attend Easter Mass with them, I attend at Christmas with them at home. And when I go to Mexico, I attend church with my grandfather, but I do that out of respect for him, I do it out of respect for my parents. I don't do it because I agree with the institution of the church. Ultimately, to me it's a bunch of white men in Europe who wrote all of those laws anyway, and I don't agree with them." Yolanda provides an unusual suggestion of Chicana feminism among local residents, though she had not grown up in this area.[43]

Despite some dissatisfaction with the Catholic Church, few local Latinas/os seem to have left it for a Protestant denomination. Candace Arroyo's mother and grandmother, who converted to Free Methodism,

[42] Arredondo, Yolanda, interview, 2003, for this and the next paragraph.
[43] See Vol. I, Ch. 6A.

were rare early exceptions.[44] Although Candace's parents had been married in the Catholic Church, she and her siblings were raised as Free Methodists. There is no indication that local Protestant churches were proselytizing among Catholics during most of the twentieth century, but by its end, a few evangelical denominations—especially in Longmont—were actively wooing Latinas/os. But even people who joined a Protestant congregation might maintain some Catholic traditions. Lucia Villagran, born in 1926 and interviewed in 2013, had stopped going to Mass at St. John's Church in Longmont in favor of an evangelical denomination, but she still continued some activities that she thought of as Mexican: celebrating Christmas on Dec. 24, making *buñuelos* for New Year's, and observing Lent by cooking fish enchiladas and lentils.[45] The association of food with religious holidays thus remained strong. By the 1980s and 1990s, however, intermarriage between Latinas/os and other ethnic groups had increased, creating more families that had mixed religious traditions or where one spouse left Catholicism to join the other's church.

Catholicism nevertheless remained a feature of many Latinas/os' lives in the decades around 2000. People commonly took older relatives to Sunday Mass. Families sometimes went to church as a group and then got together with friends or relatives afterwards at a home or restaurant. Some people were heavily involved with their parishes. Angelina Casias of Lafayette, who was nearly 70 when she described her activities in 1989, appreciated Immaculate Conception Church, especially participating in a prayer group called the "Renew Class."[46] But some religious practice still occurred at home. When 71-year-old Hank Blazón was interviewed in 2013, he displayed some of the religious objects that his family continued to treasure.[47] They included a carved wooden *santo* that his deeply religious parents used to love, which Hank and his siblings now passed around among themselves every three months, to maintain the family tradition. Arthur Perez, a much younger man, stressed how important religion was for his family.[48] "We're Catholic, it's what my family's always been. Very strong Catholic. My grandmother and my mother to this day still pray a rosary every morning." All the significant

[44] Arroyo, Candace, interview, 1977.
[45] Villagran, Lucia and Lily, interview, 2013. See also Ch. 3A above.
[46] "Casias, Angelina and Raymond, biography."
[47] "Hank Blazón showing his family's religious objects" and Blazón, William ("Hank"), interview, 2013.
[48] Perez, Arthur, interview, 2013.

religious milestones, "getting married or your first Confirmation, all these things are a big deal in our family. Celebrated with joy. God and Jesus Christ have been a big part of our family."

Yet some bitterness lingered from previous racism within the Church. One participant in the BCLHP described a conversation with a priest at Sacred Heart in Boulder about scheduling his marriage service in the church in the mid-1970s. The priest said, "You monkeys always spend too much on weddings. Why don't you just elope and save your pennies to pay off your debts?" Another participant said that although he was still nominally a Catholic, he had little respect or affection for the Church, "which has always treated us like cattle."

Although participation in parish life was limited for many Boulder County Latinas/os until at least the 1950s, being Catholic remained part of many people's identity right through the twentieth century. Religious faith was one of the legacies left by earlier Hispanics in Boulder County. Even if people did not go to Mass regularly, they rarely abandoned Catholicism for another church. The cultural and social components of religion were also important. As the Epilogue to this book suggests, spirituality still mattered to young people in 2013, though they did not always adhere strictly to the practices of their parents and grandparents.

Chapter 6

Education

Obtaining a good education for their children was a goal of most Latino parents in Boulder County throughout the period between 1900 and 1980. For people who moved here in search of "a better life," whether from Mexico, New Mexico, southern Colorado, or elsewhere, that life generally included not only improved employment opportunities for themselves and a more secure economic situation for their families, but also a chance for their children to go to school and gain the background and skills that would enable them to prosper as adults. Most parents wanted their children to stay in school as long as possible, until their labor became necessary to help support the household. Latino children faced pressure from teachers and other youngsters to speak English and adopt Anglo practices, and in some cases they experienced active discrimination. We have seen the efforts of local Chicano leaders in the 1970s to lessen racism in schools and improve conditions for all Latino students.[1] Despite the challenges children faced, quantitative evidence between 1905 and 1964 demonstrates a high level of school enrollment. This study does not support the negative stereotype that says that Latinas/os do not value education.

A. The Latino Commitment to Education

Longmont, Lafayette, and Boulder all had public schools by 1900. In none of them were Latino children denied admittance or formally segregated from Anglo ones, as was true in some borderland states.[2]

---

[1] See Vol. I, Ch. 7A.

[2] Acuña, *Occupied America*, pp. 179-180. For Colorado's state-wide educational policy and the impact of anti-immigration ordinances on equality of educational opportunities for Latinas/os, see Romero, "Of Greater Value Than the Gold of Our Mountains," and his "No Brown Towns."

But because all schooling in Boulder County was conducted by Anglo teachers in English until at least around 1970, the ability of Latino children to succeed rested upon their ability to function in that language and conform to unfamiliar cultural expectations. We do not have a full list of early schools in Longmont, but they included Columbine and later Pleasant View Ridge Elementary Schools; older children went to Central or Longmont Junior High and then Longmont High.[3] In Lafayette, the elementary school was situated next to the high school. We know more about Boulder's schools due to detailed listings in the School Census records of the 1930s, 1940s, and 1950s. In that period, most Latino elementary school children went to Lincoln or Whittier.[4] If they continued, they went to Northside Intermediate, later renamed Casey Junior High; over time, some started going on to Boulder High School.[5]

Latino children in Boulder and Longmont might have the option of attending a Catholic school. But church-run schools required payment for tuition and uniforms, whereas public schools were free. In Boulder, a handful of Latino families sent their children to Sacred Heart School in the 1930s and 1950s, with a somewhat larger number in the 1940s.[6] At that time, Sacred Heart went only through eighth grade; if children continued, they moved into the public school system, where most Latinas/os had been right along. Boulder was also the home of Mount St. Gertrude Academy, a school for wealthy Catholic girls, most of them boarders, but local families did not send their children there.[7] In Longmont, the nuns associated with St. John's Church ran a school from at least the mid-1920s.[8] Some Latino children went there for the first few years and then transferred into the public schools; a few continued at St. John's for all eight grades. In this town too, however, most children

---

[3] See "Pleasant View Ridge School, 1949, grades 1-4" and "Pleasant View Ridge Elementary, Longmont, 1949, grades 5-8." For Columbine in 2013, see "Longmont, film of places of historical importance."

[4] See "Lincoln Elementary School, Boulder, Class Pictures," "Lincoln Elementary School, Boulder, Grades 3-4," and "Parents wave goodbye to children."

[5] See "Casey Middle School, 1943, and Boulder High School, 1937" and "Boulder, film of places of historical importance."

[6] See App. 6.1.

[7] The only known exception was Teresa Alvarez, who worked at the school in the late 1940s so two of her daughters could go as day pupils (Alvarez, Teresa, interview, 1976.)

[8] In the School Census book for Longmont in 1925, 8 of the 52 children with Latino surnames attended the "Sisters" school.

attended the public schools throughout.

Parents' determination that their children should go to school is mentioned in interviews with people who came to this area early in the century as well as later arrivals. Some families chose a place to live in part because of the educational facilities of the area. Boulder was thought to offer particularly good schools, especially at the secondary level. Canuto and Gregoria Martinez left the coal mining areas of eastern Boulder County in the mid-1930s, settling themselves and their ten children in Boulder town, "because of less racial discrimination than in the surrounding communities . . . and for better educational and employment opportunities for their children."[9] Roy Maestas, who came to Boulder from Lafayette in the late 1930s, said he picked the town because of its beauty and good schools.[10] Six of his seven children went to the public schools, one to Sacred Heart. David Toledo, who had been working for some years as a miner in Erie and Frederick, brought his family to Boulder in the 1940s, where he could earn more money but also help his children get a better education.[11] He believed it was the parents' role to have enthusiasm for education and motivate their children to go to school; he disapproved of people who took their children out of school to work in the fields.

Many Latino families in Boulder's Water + Goss Streets area wanted their children to graduate from high school. David Herrera was one of the first, completing Boulder High in 1935 with an emphasis on science; Frank Madrigal graduated in 1939.[12] After that, the number of Latino graduates rose for several decades: an average of 2 or 3 per year in the 1940s, 4 per year in the 1950s, and 5 per year in the 1960s. Other graduates lived elsewhere in the town.[13] For at least a few young people, the importance of education was heightened by relatives who had been teachers. Tom Abila's grandfather was a school teacher in Walsenburg during the 1930s and 1940s, fluent in both Spanish and English.[14] As an older man he liked to take out his books and teach his grandchildren. Patrick Arroyo's father, the son of a wealthy and educated family in

---

[9] "Biographical sketch, Emma Gomez Martinez."

[10] Maestas, Roy, interview, 1978.

[11] Toledo, David, interview, c. 1978.

[12] "Graduates of Boulder Prep (High) School" and, for this and below, "Latino graduates from Boulder High School, 1935-1980."

[13] "Latino student graduates High School, 1956," "Latino student graduates High School, 1962," and "Latino students graduate High School, 1964, Pts. 1 and 2."

[14] Abila, Tom, interview, 1978.

Jalisco, Mexico that owned an import-export business, initially entered a seminary to become a Franciscan priest but then decided not to pursue that career.[15] Instead he ran a small school before moving to Colorado, where he worked as coal miner. His granddaughter described in 1977 how intelligent and well informed he was, always reading and happy to answer questions about any topic.

Yet teenagers from the Water + Goss Streets families sometimes found it hard to reconcile their parents' emphasis on doing well in school and preparing for a better future, which might mean accommodating themselves to Anglo ways and minimizing their distinctiveness, with the ongoing warmth and vitality of the Latino culture they experienced at home and in their neighborhood.[16] The ethnic identity that started to emerge among these young people in the 1950s and early 1960s struggled with these inherent contradictions.

During the second half of the century, many Latinas/os were still determined to pursue an education, whether they came from established families or were newly arrived.[17] Edwina Salazar, later the executive Director of the OUR Center in Longmont, was born in Denver in 1948 to a family from the San Luis Valley.[18] Her father was a barber, and her mother cleaned houses. When Edwina was only four years old, her mother—who had had to leave school in eighth grade to help support her family—began to insist that she had to finish high school. "She told me that she washed floors for wealthy people for a quarter a floor, 25 cents, and that she wasn't going to have a daughter of hers end up without an education. That was always a vivid memory of mine." Her mother became ill when Edwina was 11 and died when she was 14, leaving her daughter with that insistence that she had to get an education. And so she did. After high school Edwina worked in the defense industry in California and then attended Colorado State University where she obtained a Bachelor's degree and a Master's degree in Social Work. When Olga Melendez Cordero's father and uncle brought their families to Longmont from Mexico in the 1960s, Olga, her four sisters, and her six cousins all went to school, where "our teachers loved us. We knew how to behave and how to treat people because our parents had taught us

---

[15] Arroyo, Candace, interview, 1977.
[16] See Vol. I, Ch. 5C.
[17] For a belief in education among some young immigrants in 2013, see the Epilogue below.
[18] Salazar, Edwina, interview, 2013.

how to be."[19] After getting a college degree, Olga worked as a counselor at Skyline High School in Longmont. In 2009 two of her sisters had their own businesses and another was a teacher; among her cousins were a physical therapist, a physician's assistant, and a speech therapist.

Some Latinas/os obtained or completed their education only as adults.[20] Elvinia ("Bea") Martinez Borrego was never able to attend school as a child in New Mexico in the 1910s, because she had to help her father and stepmother with their work.[21] But although she had no formal education at all, as an adult she taught herself to read and write (enjoying especially the *Longmont Times-Call* and reading aloud to her grandchildren), as well as how to drive, bank, and take care of the family finances. Opportunities for adult education expanded as the result of Office of Economic Opportunity programs in the later 1960s and 1970s.[22] Diana Arroyo of Boulder, aged 45, who had previously run a daycare center at her house and babysat children, was enrolled in a Manpower training program run by the OEO in 1977. She was taking courses in secretarial skills and accounting that would qualify her for work in a bank.[23]

Mary Martinez, who lived with her grandparents in Milliken after her mother died, said in a 1988 interview that she had always wanted to be a nurse, from the time she was a child.[24] But while working in the fields, she asked herself, "How can I ever become a nurse?" for she knew you had to have a high school degree and she had only gone through eighth grade. She married at age 19, and when her children were older, she decided to prepare for some kind of job. She saw a notice in the Longmont newspaper saying, "Would you like to be a nurse?" and looked into it. She found that you could become a nurse's aide with only 100 hours of training; within one month she had completed those hours at what is now Longmont United Hospital. Although she loved going to work every day and made friends with the people she helped, she realized after a year that she was almost doing the work of a Licensed Practical Nurse (LPN). When she commented that she would like to gain that

[19] Cordero, Olga Melendez, interview, 2009.

[20] For another example, see Esther Blazón in Vol. I, Ch. 6C.

[21] "Borrego, Albert and Elvinia ("Bea") Martinez, biography."

[22] For the OEO and its impact, see Vol. I, Ch. 6C. For programs at the University of Colorado, see Vol. I, Ch. 7B.

[23] Arroyo, Candace, interview, 1977.

[24] Martinez, Mary, interview, 1988, for this paragraph.

training, her supervisor came to her and encouraged her to join the LPN course offered by the Boulder Valley School District. Shortly thereafter the President of the Lions Club, who worked at the hospital, called her into his office and said that his group had awarded her a scholarship for LPN training. Thrilled, Mary went to sign up for the course but was told she needed a high school diploma. A school counselor encouraged her to take the GED test, which she did and passed, at age 42. She then completed the nurses' training course, becoming the first Latina in the county to graduate as an LPN. She worked at the Longmont hospital for many years, teaching Latino and Anglo parents about child health and putting on an annual Mexican dinner; later she served on the Colorado State Board of Volunteers.

B. Racism and Discrimination at School

The eagerness of Latino parents to send their children to school, and the willingness of children to stay there, becomes more impressive when one recognizes the special challenges these youngsters faced in an Anglo educational system. Some of the problems stemmed from where families lived and the regularity with which children could attend school, but others resulted from the expectations and assumptions of their teachers. While some teachers were described in interviews as having been sympathetic and helpful to children from a different cultural background, the narratives provide many accounts of racist attitudes and sometimes active discrimination on the part of Anglo teachers and children.

Some obstacles that confronted Latino children were practical. The children of farm workers often lived some distance from the nearest school, and there were no school buses.[25] Shirley and Angela Vigil walked 2 miles each way to get to Hygiene elementary school from the farm where they were living in the late 1940s.[26] Other agricultural families moved to different farms within a given area over the course of the growing season. Virginia Maestas went to several schools each year as a young child in the late 1930s.[27] She and her brothers walked to school, regardless of the weather, and they ate their lunches outside since they

[25] For the special problems faced by migrant workers' children, see Vol. I, Ch. 6B.
[26] Vigil, Jennie, and others, interview, 2001.
[27] Maestas, Virginia, interview, 2013.

were the only Latino children.

More serious problems grew out of language and cultural differences. One arose the minute children enrolled in school: what were their names? Many children had Spanish first names that were at least unfamiliar and sometimes religiously uncomfortable for their teachers. When they entered school, therefore, they were normally given an Anglo equivalent, which often stuck with them for life. Jennie Vigil, born in 1919, was originally named Juanita, but when she started school the teachers changed her name.[28] Jessie Velez Lehmann, who was baptized Jesus, was told that it was a boy's name and not appropriate on religious grounds anyway, so she was enrolled as Jessie.[29] Sally Martinez, who started school at the Serene camp near the Columbine Mine in the 1920s, did not even know that her baptismal name was Celenez until many years later, when she needed to get a copy of her birth certificate for a passport.[30] When one looks down the list of first names of Latino-surnamed children in School Census records, it seems highly likely that names like Tom, Joe, Frank, and Susie had not been awarded at the child's birth. Although teachers probably felt that they were helping the children assimilate to American patterns, which would make it easier for them to succeed, some Latinas/os felt in retrospect that having been required to change their names was an attack on their cultural identity.

Language was often a barrier. Communication with teachers was difficult for parents who did not speak English and who did not know how local schools functioned and what their expectations were. Dora Bernal of Boulder spoke only Spanish though she had lived in Boulder County for many years. When asked in 1978 if she had ever been invited to school to talk with her children's teachers, Dora replied, "Yes, they invited us. But I never understood why. I never went."[31] Notes sent home in English were meaningless to her. When parents did to go to conferences with teachers, their children often had to act as interpreters, not an ideal situation.

Language problems were more severe for the children themselves. Many Latino youngsters knew little if any English when they started school. Until around 1970 and in some cases long after that, the standard

---

[28] Vigil, Jennie, and others, interview, 2001.
[29] "Los Inmigrantes."
[30] "Salazar, Jose Benito and Isabelle, biography." For the Columbine Mine, see Vol. I, Chs. 3B and 4A.
[31] Bernal, Dora, interview, 1978, a translated version.

approach was that children were prohibited from speaking Spanish, even on the playground, so as to learn English most quickly. Until they could function in English, teachers made no attempt to teach them in their own language. That policy—and the penalties used to enforce it—were remembered with considerable bitterness by many Latinas/os. Emma Gomez Martinez later wrote that her parents enrolled her and her sister Julia in school together in Erie in the early 1930s, when they were aged five and six. The girls did not speak English, and their parents "knew discrimination was strong and we could support each other."[32] After having their hands slapped with a ruler for speaking Spanish, Emma and Julia quickly learned not to use their first language at school. Cleo Estrada, who grew up in the San Luis Valley, was upset by an even stronger punishment: "Some Latino boys were lined up in front of the class one day and spanked for speaking Spanish."[33] That made Cleo decide to stop speaking Spanish herself. It "left such an impression on me that I've had to struggle to maintain my level of Spanish expertise since."

Lack of competence in English could be read by teachers as lack of intelligence. Virginia Maestas learned only minimal English in the first schools she attended, nor did she learn to read, for there were no bilingual programs.[34] When she entered a two-room school east of Boulder on a more regular basis, she had a lot of headaches, due to the pressure of trying to function in English. "I'm sure I knew some very fundamental, basic kinds of things like 'Good morning,' or 'I got to go to the bathroom.' But it wasn't until fourth grade that a teacher finally decided that since I could reason numbers, I must also be able to function in other ways mentally, academically."[35] That teacher brought Virginia home and told her mother that Virginia and her brother were not stupid, they were just hampered by lack of English. The teacher then "took it upon herself to teach my younger brother, who is two years younger than I am, and myself to read."

An assumption that Latino children, even those who spoke English, were not smart enough to function well in regular classrooms was still present in the second half of the twentieth century. In 1967, while Emma Gomez Martinez was working for the Office of Economic Opportunity

---

[32] "Martinez, Emma Gomez, letter to her children." For Emma's history, see Vol. I, Ch. 6C.
[33] "Estrada, Cleo, autobiographical information."
[34] Maestas, Virginia, interview, 2013. For Virginia's later career, see Vol. I, Ch. 6C.
[35] Maestas, Virginia, interview, 1978.

in Boulder, she enrolled her youngest daughter and a niece, both of whom were fluent in English, in the kindergarten at Lincoln Elementary School.[36] When Emma was at the school a few days later, helping other Latino parents to enroll their children, "I looked into the classroom and didn't see the girls. I asked, 'Where are they?' I was escorted to another classroom and informed that the class was for emotionally and learning disabled children. They had placed them in that federally funded class without testing or parent notification." Within days, Emma had arranged for the kindergarten class—including her girls—to be bused to a different school, where they were all treated as regular students. When Carmen Ramirez and her husband, both professional people, moved to Longmont in 1991, her nine-year-old daughter, who spoke good English and Spanish and was doing well in school, was put into a Special Education classroom.[37] Carmen was told it was standard practice for all Latino children coming from Texas or Florida. Only after vigorous objection from Carmen was her daughter moved into a regular classroom. Being treated as intellectually inferior must have damaged many children's self-esteem and confidence, weakening their ability to do well academically.

Another common assumption was that Latino children were dirty and likely to carry head lice. When Emma Gomez and her sister were in second grade, the school nurse checked for lice.[38] Emma and Julia were not examined, however: the nurse instead pinned a note on their clothes and sent them home. In a later letter, Emma described what happened next:

> The note informed my parents that Julia and I had lice and could not attend school until we were inspected by a doctor who said we were clean. My mom took a look at the note; she whipped off her apron and called the neighbor to watch the baby. She took us each by the hand and walked us back to school, up the west steps and through the hall to the principal's office. She then confronted the principal and the nurse and told them, "I will sit on this chair and any lice you find on my girls, I'll eat right here!" Apologies were all over the place. I am so proud of my mom to this day.

An equation between Latino children and head lice emerged a

---

[36] "Martinez, Emma Gomez, letter to her children."
[37] Ramirez, Carmen, interview, 2013.
[38] "Martinez, Emma Gomez, letter to her children," for this and below.

generation later in the nearby town of Frederick.[39] When an outbreak of lice occurred in 1976, only the "Mexican" girls and boys were checked at first. Secundino Herrera, a member of the Parents Committee for Equality of Education in the district, acted as a mediator between parents and school officials. He went to the administrators, whom he regarded as "narrow minded and inconsistent," and asked them to show him the lice, which they had in a little box. He then challenged them to say which of the lice were Mexican. "They couldn't answer me. I told them that there were *piojos* [lice] in the school alright—there was no doubt about it, but that they shouldn't just blame the *mejicanos* for that."[40]

Another stereotype on the part of some school staff was that Latinas/os were unambitious and unlikely to succeed. Patsy Cordova remembered that when she was in junior high school in Longmont in the early 1960s, a counselor pulled her aside, thinking she was an Anglo. He told her

> I was never going to get anywhere running around with riffraff. When I asked him what he meant, he said, "Mexicans. The Mexicans are underachievers, they're lazy, they don't care, and you stick around with them and you'll never get anywhere. They'll pull you down to their level. So, Pat, I'm giving you a piece of advice. Don't hang around with the Mexicans."[41]

Patsy recalled, "I was confused because I was raised a Mexican, and this man was telling me how terrible we are. It hurt, because I could never see my mom and dad in that light."

The expectation among teachers and counselors that Latino children would not get ahead led to lack of encouragement for them to stay in school, much less to think about higher education. Absence of guidance and support contributed in turn to a high dropout rate, which was also fueled in some cases by a practical need to start working to help their families. When Emma Gomez was in elementary school in the 1930s, about half of the children were Spanish speakers.[42] By eighth grade, however, there were just three Spanish-speaking girls, one Spanish-speaking boy, and Emma and her sister Julia. Of the six, only the Gomez girls and one other completed high school. "In those 12 years of school, not once were we counseled to higher grades." But because Emma's parents valued education highly, she and her five siblings all graduated

---

[39] Herrera, Secundino, interview, c. 1987.
[40] Ibid.
[41] Cordova, Patsy, interview, c. 1987.
[42] "Martinez, Emma Gomez, letter to her children."

from high school. In Boulder, Dixie Lee Aragon, who later had a long career as a court administrator and businesswoman, was at Casey Junior High in 1961-2. Her counselor insisted that she go to the Vocational-Technical School next ("that was where all Mexicans went"), even though Dixie told her she planned to go to college.[43] Dixie took the paperwork home, erased what the counselor had marked, added her own plans, and had her mother sign it. She then entered the college preparatory course at Boulder High and graduated with a scholarship to the University of Colorado.

Nor was the experience of Latino children in the parochial schools always positive. In Longmont during the 1930s, the seven children of Adela and Benjamin Vigil, who were being raised by their grandparents, attended St. John's School.[44] But the children were sent as recipients of charity and suffered for it.

> Despite their generosity of pocketbook, the benefactors lacked a generosity of spirit. They never let it be forgotten that the children attended St. John's because of them. The nuns, too, constantly reminded them that they were wards of charity. For example, the benefactress would bring clothes to the children and announce before the classroom, "These are for the Vigil children."

Phil Hernandez, when describing Sacred Heart School in Boulder during the 1950s, talked about the discrimination he and the few other Latino children had experienced at the hands of Anglo nuns, priests, and students.[45] He could not remember a single time when any of the teachers had spoken out against racism.

Some Latino children had parents who were willing to resist discrimination or at least advise them on how to deal with it. Emma Gomez's mother fought successfully against the sixth-grade teacher who was charging 10 cents from Spanish-speaking students to get their report cards, but nothing from English speakers.[46] When Eleanor Montour was in secondary school, she resented the discrimination she experienced on the part of some of her teachers, but her family kept telling her, "Don't play into their hands, don't let them make you quit

---

[43] "Racism in the school system," "Dixie Lee Aragon, honor award," and "Dixie Lee Aragon receives Gambill Scholarship."

[44] "Cortez, Jose Hilario ("J. H.") and Maria Sabina, biography," for this and below.

[45] "Boulder, film of places of historical importance."

[46] "Martinez, Emma Gomez, letter to her children."

school!"[47] At one point, when she was having trouble with a particular teacher, she went home and told her mother, Alicia Sanchez:

> "I'm not going back there anymore. I refuse to be ignored. I refuse to be treated the way I am being treated. I don't want to go to school anymore." My mother just said, "Well, you have a choice. You can either go to school by yourself, or I can go with you and sit next to you if you feel like you need that." So of course I returned to the school the next day by myself!

Challenges seem to have been greater for Latino children in junior and senior high school than when they were younger, in part because of social tension with their peers. When describing her experiences in Lafayette in the 1950s and early 1960s, Eleanor Montour said,

> There was a lot of racism, a lot of discrimination, and by junior high you learned what you should do and what you should not do, and survival skills. You had teachers that when you raised your hand and had an answer to a question would not acknowledge you. Not being invited to the sleepovers, not being part of many of the social things that were going on at the schools. So I had two different lives. I had my life at high school where I went and I studied and I did what I was supposed to. And then I had a life with Latinos who had dropped out of school—many of them because they had to work to help their families. So I was like two different people.[48]

Peer interactions across ethnic lines could indeed be difficult, even when other children were welcoming. Virginia Maestas described the culture shock she experienced when her family moved to Boulder in 1945, having previously been farm workers. She went from small rural schools to Casey Junior High, where she was overwhelmed by its size, large classes, and her ongoing handicap at functioning in English.[49] But the social component was equally problematic. When she was in eighth grade, she was invited to a slumber party for the birthday of an Anglo girl whose father was a judge. Virginia had never been to a slumber party before, and her mother bought her a pair of pajamas, another first. (Her mother was obviously willing to have Virginia participate in Anglo social

---

[47] Montour, Eleanor, interview, 2013, for this and below. Alicia Sanchez was the founder of the Clinica Campesina (see Ch. 3B above); Sanchez Elementary School in Lafayette is named in her honor ("Lafayette, film of places of historical importance").

[48] Montour, Eleanor, interview, 2013. She said that the Latino students sat together at lunch for defense. "If we were together as a unit then we couldn't be bothered, we couldn't be hassled."

life.) When Virginia walked into the girl's house, she was amazed to see how many things they had in it. Further, the other girls had brought their own sleeping bags, but she did not have one. She felt totally out of place and asked to go home. When she was later asked by that girl to another event, she did not accept. "I didn't want to be among white people again." Her two older brothers had so much trouble adjusting to Boulder and its overwhelmingly Anglo culture that they spent much of their time in the southern San Luis Valley with their grandparents.

Tom Abila described a similar transition. His family moved to Boulder in 1947 from a small farming community that was almost entirely Spanish-speaking. He enrolled in Casey Junior High, where he had to take English language classes after school. When asked in 1978 what Casey had been like, he replied: "I felt lost actually. Not only coming from a Chicano family, the community itself. You know, I was brought up on a farm and I wasn't used to a lot of people, big buildings, and big places, stuff like that. I was completely lost, really."[50] He said the few other Latino children (he remembered only five other families) were helpful to him, as were two or three of his teachers, but he had trouble communicating with most of the staff. Of the Anglo children, "Some were nice, some were not so nice, and some were hateful. It took me a year or so to get over that."

Even without a rural-urban transition, economic and cultural contrasts between Latino and Anglo families could be painful for young people. A participant in the Boulder Hispanic Families project of 2012 who had grown up in the Water + Goss Streets neighborhood, wrote, "It was difficult to sit in a classroom at Boulder High School and listen to your classmates talk about their parents' business trip to Sweden, when your father is the custodian at the middle school and only has a third grade education. The disparity was obvious, but the contributions and value of my father were not appreciated. How do you make a community aware that one man's hard work and sacrifices were the building blocks for a better future for his children?"[51]

By the 1960s and 1970s, Latino young people were becoming more accepted and integrated in some schools, thanks in part to sports. Linda Arroyo-Holmstrom painted a positive picture of Boulder High in those decades.[52] The school had "a place for everybody," with Latinos well

[49] Maestas, Virginia, interview, 2013.
[50] Abila, Tom, interview, 1978.
[51] An unidentified statement in a draft application for funding for the project.
[52] "Boulder, film of places of historical importance," which also shows the school in 2013.

represented in clubs and organizations. Although there were few Latino students (only 5–10 graduated each year), they included some successful athletes who went on to state level competitions. Some were even chosen as "Club Sweethearts" at dances! Linda was, however, atypically well acculturated to Anglo society: not all Latinas/os in Boulder County would have described their high school experiences in such rosy terms.

Even in the later twentieth century, third- or fourth-generation Latino children were sometimes caught in the middle between two cultures. Arthur Perez, born in 1981 to a family that had lived in Boulder County since the 1930s, was challenged as a child after moving to Italian/Anglo Louisville, "What are you doing in this playground? You don't belong here. Your kind doesn't belong here."[53] He commented in 2013, "It was very shocking. Even as an eight-year-old, you just don't even know what to say. Or do. A very uncomfortable feeling—to have hatred towards you for no reason." Yet as a young adult he was sometimes criticized by "my own culture because I don't speak Spanish. Or I don't talk with an accent, a thick accent, a lot of times. Or with a Chicano twang all the time. I've definitely been ridiculed for that." Functioning well within Anglo society while still being accepted by Latino peers could be difficult.

C. Quantitative Information

In addition to the quantitative information presented in Volume I about immigration patterns of Latino-surnamed school children and their parents, we have some evidence about the literacy and educational levels of adults and the grades and ages of children between 1905 and 1964. Rebecca Chavez's detailed analysis of the U.S. Census records for Longmont, 1920–1940, shows a higher level of literacy and ability to speak English among these early arrivals than might have been expected, though some respondents may have shaped their answers to sound as anglicized and educated as possible.[54] In 1920, the first year in which more than a few Latinas/os lived in the town, 64% of the men and 48%

---

[53] Perez, Arthur, interview, 2013. In Louisville, unlike Lafayette, people from Italian backgrounds came to be regarded as white, whereas Hispanics were brown and more heavily discriminated against (see Vol. I, Ch. 1A).

[54] Calculated from figures produced by Rebecca Chavez—and generously made available to the BCLHP—for her "Making Them Count." See "U.S. Census Records for Longmont," 1920, 1930, and 1940 for the raw data.

nformation was recorded said they were able
930, the figures had risen to 72–73% for both
Latinos and 51% of the Latinas spoke English,
d 73% of the women in 1930. The U.S. Census
t information, reporting the highest grade of
pleted. An interesting feature of these figures
nilar for Latino men and women, rather than
nal advantage for males:

	Men	Women
at all	25%	28%
	24%	19%
	28%	30%
	18%	16%
	5%	7%
	1%	--- [55]

Quantitative evidence about Latino children's participation in
Boulder County's schools has been gathered from the annual Census
reports required of every school in Colorado from sometime in the
late nineteenth century through 1964.[56] The School Census books give
each student's name, birthdate, and grade, sometimes with additional
information, including their ethnicity or nationality. The BCLHP's
volunteers analyzed a sample of School Census records for Longmont,
using the middle year of each decade, 1905–1955, plus the final year
of these books. For Lafayette and Boulder, whose surviving records are
spottier, we have information for only three or four decades. Included in
the databases are children with Latino surnames (or whose names were
known to belong to local Latino families) and those whose nationality
or ethnicity was said to be "Spanish" or "Mexican" in years when it was
stated. This quantified information is unusual: the potential of School
Census records for studying children from under-represented groups
has not been generally recognized.[57]

We may start with Longmont, where an early Latino commitment to
education is clearly visible. In 1925, 52 children from 27 Latino families
were enrolled in local schools.[58] Because the 1920 U.S. Census for

[55] Calculated from "U.S. Census Records for Longmont, 1940."
[56] See Vol. I, Ch. 2D and Apps. 2.2, 2.3, and 2.4 for a description of these records and the
information they provide about immigration.
[57] For exceptions, see Taylor, *Mexican Labor*, e.g., Tables 4-5, and Donato, *Mexicans and
Hispanos*, e.g., Table 4.2.
[58] See Vol. I, App. 2.2. For Census figures, see Vol. I, App. 3.2.

Longmont includes only 31 households with any Latino residents, this suggests that the great majority of them were already sending at least some of their children to school. Then as later, more girls were in school than boys, presumably because within a population composed primarily of agricultural workers, the labor of young males was more valuable to the family than that of females. That sex distribution contrasts with the more even number of boys and girls within the student body as a whole.

Similar proportions are seen later. By 1935, 72 Latino families in Longmont had children in school, in comparison to the 79 households listed in the U.S. Census for 1930.[59] In 1945, just over 100 families had school children, as compared to 103 households in the U.S. Census for 1940. The proportion of Latino children in the Longmont schools was also rising. In 1935, the 162 Latinas/os constituted 6% of the total enrolment; between 1945 and 1964, the 228–550 children formed 10% of the total. This evidence indicates that right from the start, Longmont's Latino parents wanted some children to receive an education even when they could have been useful in the fields.

The figures look rather different for Boulder and Lafayette.[60] The Latino percentage of all children enrolled in Boulder was tiny: not more than 3% even in 1955. If only a small fraction of all the students were Latino, the children may well have felt conspicuous and marginalized among a large mass of Anglo children. In Lafayette, by contrast, the proportion of Latino children rose steadily from 1915 onward: 12% in 1925, 22% in 1935, and 31% in 1944. When one out of every three or four children was Latino, they went through school with lots of peers and the emotional support gained from being with students from similar backgrounds.

In turning to the grade levels of Latino school children, we see a gradual increase in the percentages that went beyond sixth grade.[61] A rising level of education across time was common among many immigrant groups in the United States. In Boulder County, the fraction of Latino children in seventh and eighth grades increased first, followed by the fraction in senior high school. As early as 1935, 12%–13% of Latino children in Lafayette and Boulder public schools were in grades 9–12, with a much lower proportion in Longmont. By 1945, Longmont had risen to 12% of Latino students in senior high school, and Boulder had

---

[59] See Vol. I, Apps. 2.2 and 3.2, for this and below.
[60] See Vol. I, App. 2.3.
[61] See App. 6.1.

reached the startling level of 53%. The latter figure suggests that the small number of Latino families in Boulder were determined that their children should take full advantage of the access to a good education offered by the university town. In Longmont in 1955 and 1964, the proportion of Latino students in grades 9–12 was 18%–20%, but they did not all complete high school and graduate.[62]

The ages of Latino school children show several interesting features.[63] The increase over time in the percentage of those children who were older than 12 years suggests that more parents could now afford to allow their children to continue their educations, rather than having to start work as soon as possible. Quite surprising is the proportion of Latino children in school who were aged 16 years and older. Since the official minimum age for leaving school in Colorado was no more than 15 until 1971, these older children were not legally required to stay in school. Some of them were in senior high school, but others were in lower grades, suggesting that they had not been able to go to school when they were younger and were now trying to catch up. In 1935, 26%–30% of Longmont and Lafayette's Latino school children were aged 16 or more, as were 18% in Boulder. Ten years later, the proportion of these young people was around a third in both Longmont and Boulder. The fraction dropped a little in Longmont in the mid-1950s but reached 55% in Boulder, with virtually identical proportions for both boys and girls. Some of these older students may have intended to go on to some kind of post-secondary training. In Longmont, the fraction of Latino children aged 16 or more had dropped to under a quarter by 1964, suggesting either that more children were now both starting and finishing school at the normal ages or that older teens no longer saw education as useful.

It is even more unexpected to see how many Latinas/os were still enrolled in school at ages 19–21. Their presence suggests a serious dedication to getting an education on the part of young adults as well as sufficient economic resources to free them from full-time work. As early as the mid-1920s, nearly a third of the Latina students in Longmont were aged 19 or more, with figures between 8% and 20% common for male students then and in all three towns during the following decades.[64] But

[62] Donato found only two Mexican/Hispano graduates of Longmont High School in 1935, three in 1950, two in 1955, and one in 1960, with none in the 1920s or 1940s (*Mexicans and Hispanos*, p. 84).

[63] See App. 6.2.

[64] See App. 6.2.

in Boulder in 1955, 42% of the male Latino students and 34% of the females were in this older age bracket. Many of them were probably preparing to apply to the University of Colorado. Even marriage did not necessarily stand in the way of continuing one's education. Two sets of Longmont records indicate whether female students were married. In 1925, 5 of the 8 older girls were married, as were 11 of 64 in 1964.

Access to formal education had the potential to undermine traditional family relationships. Although many Latino immigrants saw the education of their children as an opportunity to be seized as fully as possible, schooling often meant that young people gained certain kinds of knowledge and social experience beyond what their parents possessed. Children who went past a lower elementary education must have been able to read and write at least basic English and do simple mathematics. They had also learned how to survive socially within classrooms controlled by Anglo teachers and filled mainly with Anglo peers, settings that promulgated Anglo values. Many parents apparently felt they could still maintain their own position within the family while valuing the skills that enabled their children to operate more successfully in an Anglo-dominated world.

Some parents obviously wanted their daughters to be educated, not just their sons. Female education introduced the possibility of even greater dislocation within Latino families. Young women who had been to school were better positioned to function in the wider community than were those fathers and husbands who were comfortable only in Spanish and might be no more than minimally literate. By the 1940s, some women were taking paid employment that required skills gained at school. But here too, female education and the doors it opened seem to have been accepted in at least some cases as a contribution to the well-being of the family as a whole, rather than viewed as a threat to male dominance or the control of older relatives.

It should be noted, however, that although many first- and second-generation Latino families in Boulder County were committed to education as a way to help their children live effectively in the new setting, a belief in the value of schooling was not always equally strong in the third and fourth generations. Later in the twentieth century, although most Latino youngsters went to school until they were 16 or 17, as required by Colorado law from 1971 onward, they did not all graduate. In the 1970s, the dropout rate was higher among Latino children than among Anglos in both of the county's school districts.[65] For some young Latinas/os, continuing in school was no longer viewed as the pathway to a better future.

The information presented here flies in the face of the assumption that Latino immigrants did not care about education. A determination to get children educated—seen among parents and young people themselves— seems especially admirable in light of the discrimination experienced by many Latino children in school. As we shall see, the young interns who worked with the BCLHP in 2013 shared the assumption that a good education was a necessary prerequisite to the adult lives they hoped to lead. The primary difference between them and earlier arrivals was that access to higher education was now available even to first-generation immigrants, whereas previously that level was rarely attained before the third generation.

---

[65] See Vol. I, Ch. 7A. In 2012, only 67% of Latino students in the St. Vrain Valley School District and 78% in the Boulder Valley School District graduated from high school within four years; for Anglo students, the comparable figures were 86% and 93% (*Boulder County TRENDS 2013*, p. 23).

Epilogue

Echoes of the Past, Voices of the Future:
Ten Young Latinas/os in 2013-2014

We end by skipping 30 years forward in time to learn about the experiences of 10 young Latinas/os who worked as interns with the Boulder County Latino History Project in the summer of 2013. In their interviews and written statements, these outstanding high school and college students—seven women and three men—discussed many of the topics examined in the two volumes of this set. Because the interns are likely to become leaders of their communities, their descriptions of their own lives, some of them painful to read, connect the past and the present and give us hope for the future.

All of the interns were recommended by people who had worked with them at their schools or colleges or in community organizations. In the summer of 2013, four were attending local high schools or had just graduated; six were students at nearby colleges and universities or had just finished.[1] As it became clear that the interns had extremely interesting histories of their own, the BCLHP arranged for them to do videographed interviews with each other.[2] In the summer of 2014, five of them returned questionnaires that provided further information.[3]

[1] The high school students attended Skyline High School in Longmont (2), Longmont High School (1), and Centaurus High School in Lafayette (1). The older interns were undergraduates at Front Range Community College in Longmont (1), the University of Colorado at Denver (1), Metropolitan State University in Denver (1), and the University of Colorado at Boulder (3), all majoring in Ethnic Studies, of whom 2 had just graduated with honors or highest honors).

[2] All of the interns gave written permission for their interviews to be posted on the website of the Maria Rogers Oral History Program at the Carnegie Branch Library for Local History, Boulder Public Library. Nine of them were willing to have their real names used in this book; the URLs for their interviews are given in the listing of primary sources at the back: Ana Gonzalez Dorta, Ana Karina Casas Ibarra, Veronica Lamas, Deisy de Luna, Emmanuel Melgoza, Jason Romero, Jr., Dalia Sanchez, Kelly Sarceno, and Salvador Serrano. One intern requested that a substitute name be used in the book; she appears here as "Elvira Lucero."

[3] Gonzalez Dorta, Lamas, de Luna, Melgoza, and Romero. The statements described below are all found in their interviews or "Intern questionnaires" and will not be individually referenced.

Illus. Epilogue.1. *Interns and the author at a reception for BCLHP, August, 2013 back, left to right: Jason, Salvador, Emmanuel; front, left to right; Deisy, Ana Karina, Dalia, Kelly, Marjorie, Elvira, Ana, Veronica*

This epilogue reports on their experiences with immigration, employment, family relationships, religion, ethnic identities, education, discrimination, and deportation.

Nine of the interns' parents were immigrants to this country. Their histories bear striking similarities to those of the Hispanics who came to Boulder County prior to 1940. Most of their parents had left their homes elsewhere due to extreme poverty, political unrest, and/or a strong desire to create better opportunities for themselves and their children, which included getting an education. Seven of the interns were from Mexican backgrounds, in all cases from the same states that had provided immigrants early in the twentieth century. Four were born in Mexico—two in Zacatecas, one in Guanajuato, and one in Michoacán. Their parents were evidently undocumented and hence subject to arrest and deportation by ICE [Immigration and Customs Enforcement].[4]

[4] The BCLHP did not ask about the interns' immigration status, but most volunteered that information in their interviews or questionnaire responses.

Three of these foreign-born young people were themselves at risk of deportation; they could not get working papers, and until 2013 they had to pay out-of-state tuition if they wanted to go to college.[5] Deisy was the only one to have applied and paid for D.A.C.A. status through the 2012 "Dream Act," which allowed her to live and work in this country legally for a two-year, renewable period.[6] The parents of three other interns had come from Guanajuato, Durango, and Jalisco, and in at least two cases were undocumented. But because these children were born in the U.S., they were citizens.

The remaining young people came from different backgrounds. Kelly's parents had emigrated from conflict-torn Guatemala to California in the late 1970s and obtained legal residency through the 1986 Amnesty Law.[7] Kelly was born in this country, so she was a citizen. Ana's family had relocated from Caracas, Venezuela, where her father operated a successful business and her mother worked for the American Embassy. They had come to this country in 2010, with the necessary permissions, because of their opposition to the current government of Venezuela. They chose Boulder due to its ready access to good universities for their three children. Only Jason came from a deeply rooted American family. His grandparents were from old northern New Mexican families but had moved to Pueblo, in southern Colorado, where he grew up.

Current U.S. policies and practices concerning immigration, as enforced by the border patrol, have created dangerous conditions for desperate people trying to cross the border from Mexico without papers. In her interview, Ana Karina described how she walked across the desert from Mexico with her mother and two little brothers when she was 11 years old. Her mother, who was escaping from an abusive marriage in Zacatecas, had tried to cross previously with only the boys but was stopped and sent back. The next time she decided to bring Ana

[5] The passage of Colorado's ASSET bill in April of that year allowed many undocumented college students who met certain criteria to qualify for in-state tuition, which was far less expensive, though they were still ineligible for most scholarships.

[6] The federal Deferred Action for Childhood Arrivals program allowed some young people who had been brought to this country as children, without papers, to obtain permission to remain. The cost was high, however: $465 for the application, plus whatever a lawyer's fees might be.

[7] The Immigration Reform and Control Act (IRCA) of 1986 made it illegal to hire undocumented immigrants and required employers to determine their workers' immigration status, but it also granted legal status to about 3,000,000 immigrants who currently lacked formal permission to live and work in this country.

Karina too, but once again they were caught. Finally, after sleeping on the streets of a Mexican border town for several nights waiting for the *coyote* who was going to lead them across, they made it out into the desert. Ana Karina carried one of the little boys on her back much of the time. "It was really scary. . . . We were crossing through big hills full of cactus, and it was at night so we couldn't see. People were getting cactus spines all over their bodies and hands. We walked for a couple days. My mom was alone, but she got help from the other people." When they reached the other side, "We waited a long time until it got dark and a van picked us up. They took us to a house, and it was packed, packed with people." After that they were taken to Nevada and eventually came to Boulder.

In terms of employment, the fathers of those interns who had recently come from Mexico faced a somewhat wider range of options in the U.S. than had their predecessors a century before. But the jobs they found were nevertheless unskilled, poorly paid, often temporary, and—for those who were undocumented—had to be arranged and paid under the table. In time, however, some were able to move into more regular positions. Emmanuel's father, who had been a baker and very small farmer in Mexico, worked in construction when he first came to Colorado; later he was the cook in a restaurant and then became the janitor at a casino. Deisy's father had run a hamburger and Taco stand and worked in a carpet factory in Mexico. In Colorado, he first did any kind of manual labor he could find but was then hired part-time at a horse ranch and by 2013 was working there full-time, dealing mainly with the machinery. After starting with various unskilled jobs, Salvador's father took short-term factory work before getting a position at Fresca Foods.[8] Veronica's father had done factory, agricultural, and construction work in Mexico. After coming to the U.S., he was for many years a migrant farm worker, moving around with his wife and four children through Oregon, Idaho, Nevada, Colorado, and Texas. Later he did construction work.

For educated people with citizenship or papers, the options were far greater. Ana's parents had set up a business in Boulder similar to the one they had in Caracas, providing advertising and promotional materials for companies and organizations. Jason's father was an operating room assistant at a hospital, and his mother was a school nurse: he referred to

[8] When he was unemployed during the economic downswing of 2008, the whole family made and sold tamales to get by.

his family as middle class.

The mothers of the interns had generally not worked before coming to this country, and if they were currently married, a few continued as housewives. But women on their own and some of the newer immigrant wives needed to earn money. Possibilities were even more limited for them. Several cleaned houses, taking their children with them if they had no relatives to look after them. One did domestic work in a hotel, and another was employed at a *tortillaria*. Veronica's mother, who did migrant field work with her husband for some years, was later a house cleaner and eventually found a production job at a Coca-Cola bottling plant.

Thanks to their access to higher education, the interns foresaw a much wider range of possible careers than had been open to their parents. These positions would have been inconceivable for first- or second-generation immigrants early in the twentieth century. No gender differences were visible: all the Latinas expected to have their own careers, generally as professionals, like their male counterparts. Three of the young people wanted to become teachers or counselors: Ana Karina hoped to work with troubled children/teens and Elvira to teach in a bilingual school; Jason planned to start with high school teaching but later get a Ph.D. and become a professor of Chicano Studies. Veronica was determined to go to Law School and become an immigration lawyer; Kelly wanted to work on immigration reform in some capacity. The other career choices were scattered: Salvador was interested in architecture, Deisy in accounting and marketing, and Ana in film making. Dalia wanted either to become a mortician and eventually a coroner or go into the military. Emmanuel hoped to go to graduate school in political science and perhaps try politics.

When asked whether they thought that being Latino would stand in the way of their career goals, most of the interns said it would not. They did not expect to be discriminated against, and they thought that being bilingual, as all of them were, would be an asset in the kind of work they hoped to pursue. That positive hope for the future was at odds with the negative treatment many of them had already received, based upon their ethnicity.

Many of the family patterns we observed prior to 1980 remained strong for these young Latinas/os. Although the number of children per family was now much lower, close relations with grandparents were still very important. When Salvador's family first came to Colorado, they stayed with their grandmother, who had moved here earlier. He said that his grandparents "have been taking care of me since I was young. They're always striving to make me go to a higher level than them. They always tried to give me the best. I appreciate that." When both of Veronica's parents were arrested and imprisoned, she and her younger brother lived with their grandmother in Denver for three years. Elvira's grandmother stepped in to help Elvira and her mom after her dad was taken by ICE and held for deportation. Family mattered to young people from long-established American backgrounds too. Jason said that his grandparents lived near where he grew up in Pueblo, and he saw them regularly; three or four times each year his immediate family traveled to New Mexico and other parts of Colorado to visit his aunts, uncles, and cousins. For a few years, two young cousins lived with his family before moving in with his grandparents, and his aunt and her four children also lived with them temporarily.

But migration might cut ties across generations. Because people without papers could not risk crossing the border, they were unable to go to their home countries to visit relatives. Deisy said that when she lived in Mexico, "I would see my grandparents and cousins on a daily basis; my cousins were my friends, and my family was my everything." But since coming to the U.S. nine years before, she had not seen any of them in person, and it was hard to talk with them by phone. "They are family, but we live in completely different worlds." When describing life in Mexico when he was young, Emmanuel explained that while his father was away, working in the U.S., his mother and the children lived with their grandparents. "My grandparents played a big role in my childhood. They were like my parents, especially my grandfather, he was a father figure." But Emmanuel had not seen his Mexican family since he arrived in the U.S. Documented immigrants and U.S. citizens had the great advantage of being able to visit their relatives. Kelly had been to Guatemala at least ten times, Dalia visited her Mexican relatives every two years, and Ana had already returned several times to Venezuela.

In the area of religion, these young people were even more loosely connected to the Roman Catholic Church than many earlier Latinas/os. All of them were raised in Catholic families, and many had gone to church regularly with their older relatives and/or had prayers at home when they were young. Most still classified themselves generally as Catholics, and a few said they went to services anywhere between once every few weeks and once every three or four months. But several were at least partially separated from the church. Deisy, who had gone to Mass regularly with her grandfather in Mexico, commented, "I don't feel the need to go to church every week to feel spiritually bonded with God. I also believe in parts of other religions, and a 'good' Catholic does not do that. I go to church about once a month, sometimes more, sometimes none at all." Jason laid out his position more fully:

> I consider myself to be a Chicano Catholic, with many of my beliefs and practices coming from the Catholic Church. However, I also recognize the indigenous influence on my spirituality, and I enjoy exploring that further. While this is in conflict with the teachings of the Church, which claims to be the singular holy representative of God on Earth, I do embrace elements of my Native spirituality.

Defining one's identity as a Latino/a remained a problem for these young people. There was no agreement about what descriptive labels to use. Emmanuel termed himself "Mexican," and Salvador spoke about "Mexicans, whites, blacks, and Asians" as the main groups in Longmont, identifying himself with the first category. Elvira referred to people like her as "Hispanics," but Kelly talked about herself and her friends as "Latinas." Veronica described herself as "Mexican American," while Ana said she was "Venezuelan."

The degree of certainty with which the interns responded to questions about ethnicity also varied. Jason was definite in calling himself "Chicano," because he wanted to acknowledge his indigenous ancestors as well as the Spanish/European side of his background. In his interview, he described the emotional impact of reading Corky Gonzales's poem "I am Joaquín" when he was in high school, and he quoted the opening and closing lines of that powerful exploration of the various facets of Chicano identity.[9] Deisy described the complexity of her identity in a different way: "My nationality is Mexican, my ethnicity is Hispanic-Latino, and my race is white."

Dalia, however, was still struggling to situate herself. At one point in her interview she said she thinks of herself as American, because she

---

[9] "I am Joaquín, lost in a world of confusion,/ caught up in the whirl of a gringo society,/ confused by the rules, scorned by attitudes/ suppressed by manipulation, and destroyed by modern society. . . . I am the masses of my people and/ I refuse to be absorbed./ I am Joaquín./ The odds are great/ But my spirit is strong,/ My faith unbreakable,/ My blood is pure./ I am Aztec prince and Christian Christ./ I SHALL ENDURE!/ I WILL ENDURE!" (Rodolfo Gonzales, "I am Joaquín").

was born in this country, as compared to people born in Mexico. But she also talked about the social problems she faced in high school. "I wasn't Mexican enough, and I wasn't white enough either, 'cause I'll never be white enough. I was just me, stuck in the middle. I didn't know where to go or who to hang out with for a while. And then eventually, I started hanging out with the Mexicans, 'cause that was the only option I really had." When the interviewer, a slightly older intern, asked how she would describe her ethnicity, Dalia said she didn't know: "Hispanic? Both of my parents are from Mexico, so I'm Hispanic, right?"

The biggest single difference between these young immigrants and their predecessors in the first half of the twentieth century was access to high school and college education. Although previous immigrant parents were eager to have their children go to school, it was not until the 1940s that more than a few Latinas/os reached the secondary school level. Graduating from high school was common only among Latino children born in this country to well-established parents, and not until the third generation—starting in the late 1960s—did many begin to move to the college level. Among the interns, by contrast, all planned to complete high school (or had already done so) and go on for further education. Their commitment resulted in part from their parents' belief in education.

The importance of education was stressed by many of the interns. When Deisy arrived in this country from Mexico at age 13, speaking only Spanish, she went into the "Newcomers" program at Heritage Middle School in Longmont for one year, learning English. She then decided to challenge herself by transferring to Altona Middle School, where all classes were taught in English. After graduating from Silver Creek High School in Longmont, where her teachers were very supportive, she enrolled at Front Range Community College and planned to continue at the University of Colorado at Boulder [CU-Boulder]. When asked what advice she would give to other young people, she said, "Of course, go to school. Because right now, it just seems like, 'Oh, I need to work, I need to get this job, I want to buy this thing.' But in the long run, your education is the only thing that sticks with you. Education is the only thing that will save you." She remembered that when she first came to Boulder County, a man who had a job killing turkeys at the processing plant in Longmont told her to stay in school, saying "*Nunca vayas a trabajar en la mataderia.*[10] Her conclusion: "Just keep going with education is what I say, because education is the key to success."

Emmanuel described his educational history after moving to Colorado from Mexico when he was in third grade. He attended an elementary school in Denver where most of the children spoke only English.

> So it was hard for me to communicate with teachers when I needed to go to the bathroom or I needed to do something or ask a question or get help in my homework. But luckily there was a high school student who was helping ESL kids, so that's how I was able to break that barrier and start learning English . . . . I learned by reading books, by going to the library, watching a lot of TV. . . . That's how I learned English, just by listening to other people.

He had an extra reason to become competent, because his parents had little formal education and spoke almost no English: "I'm the one who's always having to take care of the bills or car companies and all those things." In middle school, he moved out of ESL classes and into regular ones; in high school he went into the International Baccalaureate program and did well in it. At the time of his interview, he had finished his second year at CU-Boulder, where he was majoring in Political Science and Ethnic Studies, with a minor in Technology, Arts, and Media.

When asked why he decided to go to college, Emmanuel said that part of the reason was to avoid "all the struggles my family has gone through, from not having food on the table, to not being able to pay bills, or having to sell items in order to pay a bill, because there's no money. Or starting to work at the age of 13." But he also felt obligated to study because other people believed in him.

> One thing my parents have taught me, "Go to college." And you know you're not the only one who's going, it's the rest of the people that are behind you, that have been supporting you all through your struggle, your teachers before, in middle school, elementary, high school, all of them. 'Cause if you fail, everybody fails. If you graduate, then you're bringing ten people with you. That's the one thing that drives me, it's them.

Veronica went to Montbello High School in Denver, in a poor community where few students even finished high school and very few went on to any kind of further education. She had a strong personal

---

[10] "I never want to see you working in the slaughterhouse."

motivation for doing well academically. When she was in elementary school, during one of the few times she saw her father in jail after his arrest and before his deportation by ICE, she said to him, "'Dad, when I grow up I'm going to become a lawyer so that I could get you out of here.' As little as I was, that's what kept me going." When she got to high school, she always told herself, "I am going to be a lawyer" and studied hard to get very good grades. She decided to go to CU-Boulder, against the advice of her teachers and counselors, who thought a community college would be the most she could handle. Veronica did come to the university but struggled in her first year because of inadequate preparation, especially in writing. When she was unhappy, her mother, who was cleaning houses at the time, encouraged her to keep trying. Veronica persevered, seeking extra help, and later graduated with Honors, having majored in Ethnic Studies, where she received good support from the faculty. She wrote her Honors thesis on the problems faced by undocumented students in obtaining a higher education.

Interns from educated, middle class families had different experiences. Jason went through the Pueblo schools and began attending Pueblo Community College while still in high school, graduating with an Associate's degree in 2010. He then went to CU-Boulder, where he graduated in 2013 with Highest Honors. Ana's family was firmly behind her education and training. She became interested in film in her early teens while living in Caracas; her parents, instead of putting on a *quinceañera* party for her, used the money to send her to a summer program in film studies in California. After the family moved to Boulder, she was involved in various film projects at Fairview High School; when she started college at the University of Colorado in Denver, she majored in film and television. While working as an intern with the Latino History Project, she made films of places in Longmont, Lafayette, and Boulder that had been important to Latinas/os.[11]

Although many local colleges and universities were trying to increase the diversity of their students in the early 2010s and therefore welcomed applications from Latino students, finances were a problem for these interns, especially those who were undocumented and therefore had to pay out-of-state tuition and/or were not eligible for scholarships. Ana Karina, who was attending Metropolitan State University in Denver on a

---

[11] "Longmont, film of places of historical importance," "Lafayette, film of places of historical importance," and "Boulder, film of places of historical importance."

part-time basis while also holding down a job, was discouraged at how slowly she was moving towards her degree. She had been paying out-of-state tuition because she was undocumented, and she could only afford to take one or two classes each semester. Some semesters she could not enroll at all. She was bitter, because although she was just as bright as other students and worked harder than most, she did not have a wealthy family who could pay her tuition, and she did not qualify for scholarships.

The interviewers asked the interns if they had experienced any form of discrimination or racism because they were Latino. A few, those with less obviously Latino skin color or features, said they had not, though they knew of others who had. The majority, however, reported that they had at times been treated differently from Anglos within the community. Salvador noticed that if he and his family went to a restaurant in Longmont, they did not get served as quickly or spoken to as nicely as the white family at the next table. Emmanuel said that in Boulder:

> You definitely get looked at weird, or with some type of face or some type of body language, when you're talking Spanish to someone.... Obviously the color that your skin is—your skin color—you stand out.... It's hard to be looked at, because we're human beings, we're not from a different world. We're the same, we're made out of bone and flesh. There's nothing different between us, it's just that they speak English, we speak Spanish, there's only that. We live in this multi-cultural country.... If we could just look at everybody as if color doesn't exist, there wouldn't be any racism in this country.

The most overt example of negative treatment evidently based on ethnicity or race was described by Jason. This case of "profiling" by the Boulder police occurred shortly after he had graduated from the University of Colorado, when he was riding one evening in his truck with a friend, who was African American. Jason drove a small, candy-apple red 1991 Chevy low rider with gold trim and lettering, an object of pride that he regarded as a statement of his cultural identity. A policeman noticed that one of Jason's headlights was out and turned on his flashing lights.

> So I pulled into a parking lot. And I kid you not, four police cars showed up. To surround one little truck, one tiny low-rider truck with two people in there, a Chicano and a black guy. But they had four police show up. They were just harassing us, asking us who we were, where we were going, what we were up to. Asking why I was dressed up at the time. (I was dressed up because I had a

presentation at work.) Asking if we had any weapons, illegal substances. Then they said, "Why are you so nervous?" They were continuously, continuously harassing us, for a good 20 minutes or so.

Eventually the police left, after explaining it was their job to keep the streets safe. "To me that's just crazy. The fact that you need four police to show up for one car." Jason was fortunate in being a citizen. Undocumented young Latinas/os were often afraid to drive—even to work—lest they be stopped for some minor problem; if they were arrested, they might be reported to ICE.

It is troubling that many of the interns had suffered racist treatment at school or college. They were generally positive about their teachers, reporting that they had helped them learn English and move into more advanced classes and had encouraged their hopes of going on to college. Deisy said that her teachers at Silver Creek High School in Longmont had even raised the money to pay for her first semester at Front Range Community College, before she was eligible to get a work-study position on campus. The interns who were undergraduates at CU-Boulder gave much of the credit for their success in staying in college to supportive professors and counselors. For Veronica, participation in the McNeill Academic Program for first-generation students made a big difference, as did the encouragement of Prof. Arturo Aldama of Ethnic Studies who advised her senior Honors thesis and backed her desire to go to Law School.

But Ana Karina felt differently. When she came from Mexico to Casey Junior High School in Boulder, not speaking any English, one of her teachers got angry and started yelling at her because she was not responding to him. Afterwards one of the Latinas she ate lunch with explained he was saying that "he couldn't understand why we were accepted into schools when we didn't speak a word of English." Later she resented how she was treated at Boulder High School.

> You feel alienated, you feel like you don't belong. Everyone, from people on the street to teachers even, they look down on you, thinking that you don't have the intelligence to do as well as a white student. And when you do actually do good, they're like, "Oh, my God, you're actually smart! Look at you!" ... It's a challenge, but it's a good challenge, because it makes us who we are. That makes us work harder and makes us stronger. We know that because we already went through so much and accomplished so many things,

the next thing to come, the next challenge, we <u>know</u> we can go through it, we can accomplish it.

Interactions with their Anglo peers at school or in college were more likely to be problematic. Kelly went to Niwot High School for her freshman year, to take advantage of its International Baccalaureate program. That school was overwhelmingly white, and she found the other students very racist. She described eating lunch in the cafeteria one day.

> It was me and my two or three friends, and we were all Latinas. We were just eating, and then one guy, he came up to us, and he was like, "Do you get free lunch?" We were like, "Yeah." And he was like, "Oh, no shock there!" There were a lot of small things like that, and it added up, and emotionally I just couldn't deal with it. So after my freshman year I went to Skyline High School. That was a better fit for me there, and I feel more accepted.

Kelly said that her teachers at Niwot sometimes tried to help. She described an incident involving her IB English teacher, "who was basically my backbone through it all." The class had an assignment of writing about themselves after reading Sandra Cisneros' *The House on Mango Street*. Kelly chose a prompt about a struggle she was dealing with, and her teacher encouraged her to write about what she was going through at school.

> I wrote about it, basically everything that really hit me hard, I just wrote it down on paper. I wrote how it was making me ashamed of who I was, and my background. That's probably one of the main reasons why I left Niwot, because I never want to feel ashamed of who I am and my background. Because my family is everything in me and my background. I'm proud of being dark skinned, having long black hair with brown eyes, and speaking Spanish. That all adds up to Kelly.

The students then read their papers out loud. Kelly was "the only girl of color, so reading that felt definitely empowering. I ended up crying, and so did my teacher, and a couple classmates did. Everyone was like, 'We didn't know just how hard it is for you' and stuff like that." She thought that other students probably realized that discrimination was an issue, but they did not want to face it.

Five of the interns had been at CU-Boulder: three as undergraduates, and two as members of a summer program for students of color between their junior and senior years in high school, designed to prepare them for college-level work and to help them and their parents navigate the process of applying for admission and financial aid. All of them commented on how difficult it was to adjust to a heavily white, English-speaking campus. Emmanuel, who had gone to high school in a largely Latino neighborhood outside Denver, observed,

> It was walking out of one bubble and walking into a different bubble without having in-between preparation. You walk into that campus, and boom, 90% white. You're used to seeing, walking down the street, it would be like, *"Hola! Como está?"* Calling out to your neighbors that speak Spanish. Walking around campus is . . . different than the way you interact back at home with your neighbor or your family.

The two high school students who had spent five weeks on the campus in CU-Boulder's Pre-Collegiate Development Program shortly before their internships were likewise struck by how few people of color there were. Elvira said, "I saw how there's very few Mexicans or Latinos in that school. It's primarily white dominant people who are there. It's scary sometimes, 'cause you don't feel comfortable where you're at, and you wish you had more people next to you with that support."

Kelly loved being on the campus, taking college classes, and meeting interesting people. But she too was startled by the shortage of students of color and the implicit prejudice her group experienced from Anglo students. The summer participants ate their meals at the university's new Center for Community, where she and her friends sat at the same table every day. Their group consisted of two Latinos (one from Mexico and herself, whose family was from Guatemala), and three students of mixed race: half black and half Latino.

> People would look at us as if we didn't belong, dirty looks. They're not saying anything, but just with their face, that says enough. Like, we don't belong here, why are you here, stuff like that. . . . That was discouraging at times. A lot of my friends, they go, "I don't want to come here 'cause there's no diversity at all." But in my head, I'm like, "If you don't come here, that's just adding to the problem, not adding the diversity that CU does need."

An important factor for the interns attending the university was participation in Latino-focused student organizations, especially UMAS y MEChA (United Mexican American Students and *Movimiento Estudiantil Chicanos de Aztlán*), the combined descendent of two groups active on campus since the 1970s.[12] Emmanuel said that joining that organization and later getting involved in student government "has opened up a different door, . . . a new chapter has started. I feel like I have a voice on campus, with being a leader and a future leader on that campus as well. There's a lot of things that need to be changed, but I feel like one foot is inside the door." Jason too described what those groups had meant to him.

> Honestly, without UMAS y MEChA, I would not have stayed at CU. I would have been gone my first semester. I remember, I was actually at a meeting with one of our professors, Dr. Aldama, and it was the very first semester of my freshman year. He said that 38% of students of color don't finish their first semester. I thought to myself, "Woa!" because I had actually been filling out my transfer paperwork to go to the University of New Mexico in Albuquerque. And I was like, "OK, well, I'm not going to be a statistic, so I've got to figure out how to make this work, how I'm going to stay." UMAS y MEChA has provided me that. It's been a community where I feel safe, where I feel like myself, where I feel like I can meet people who know who I am, who've lived similar experiences.

In conclusion, we turn to the issue of deportation. In the 1930s, some Boulder County Hispanics were subject to repatriation or deportation to Mexico.[13] It would be satisfying to end this book by saying that such treatment was no longer present in the early 2010s. Unfortunately, that is not the case. Two of the interns described the arrest and eventual deportation of their fathers by Immigration and Customs Enforcement, leaving the children—who were U.S. citizens—without emotional and financial support.

Elvira said, "Something that has impacted me in my life a lot was that last summer, my father was taken away by Immigration." Her parents were separated, and her undocumented father was living with his girlfriend Toni and her daughter. One night, when Elvira was 16, she and her younger sister were staying with their father and Toni. At 5 am, someone who looked like a policeman came to the door, asking if their parents were there. Toni's 12-year-old daughter, who answered the door, said no, for she knew that Elvira's dad had already left for work and thought that her mom had too. The officer asked when the adults would come home; when the girl said at the end of the afternoon, he

---

[12] See Vol. I, Ch. 7B.
[13] See Vol. I, Ch. 4C.

responded, "All right, I'll come back later." The girls thought he meant he would return that afternoon.

When Toni (who had actually been in the shower at the time) heard about the officer's visit and that he had a paper in his hand naming Elvira's dad, she was worried and phoned him at work. He came right home to see what was going on, and a few minutes later the officer returned. His car was parked around the corner, but Elvira could see that it said "Immigration." Her dad talked with the officer outside for a little while, handed over his credit card, ID, and wallet to Toni, and then disappeared. Shortly thereafter he phoned Toni to say that "Immigration had taken him."

Elvira continued, "A month later or so, we actually got to see him, they had him in a jail. The mirror, it's not clear, it has little black cubes, and it had that thing for you to talk, and it smells bad. You were lucky enough if you actually got the opportunity to grab a phone and talk on the phone." Elvira felt especially sad, because

> My dad, he's a working guy. They didn't allow him to do anything there. I've never seen my dad in that position. He was almost crying to me, and it broke my heart to see him like that. He was like, "I don't know what to do, there's nothing I can do here. I feel like I need to work, you guys don't have any support. Who's going to pay for your stuff?"

That worry was justified, for Elvira and her sister were now dependent on the limited earnings of their mother and their grandmother.

Elvira's dad was later moved to an immigration detention center outside Denver, run by a private company. "That was worse. Every time I kept on going [to visit him], part of me didn't want to go 'cause I knew it was going to hurt me more." When she visited, they could only see each other through computers with a camera. "That was so unfair, because . . . I couldn't grab him. I missed hugging him. It wasn't the same." At the time of her interview in 2013, Elvira's dad was still in the detention center, but she had recently been told that he was being sent to Mexico. She was worried, "'cause he's been here all his life, and he doesn't know what it's like over there."

Elvira talked about the impact of her father's arrest and disappearance on her school work. Her dad had told her when she last visited him,

> "Pretend like if I'm not here, like if nothing happened. Then you can keep on doing good in school." My teachers told me, "You

have to be strong. Just pretend everything's normal so you can continue." One of my teachers said, "I know this hurts you, but it's going to hurt him more if you don't try." So I try my best to honor him. [At that point in the interview she cried.] Things just aren't the same anymore.... I want to make 10,000 videos and put them on YouTube, to try to explain how this immigration thing is so unfair.

Veronica too saw her family ripped apart, though for somewhat different reasons. When she was seven, she, her parents, and her three siblings were staying temporarily with her grandmother in Denver. While there, both of her immigrant parents, who were in the U.S. legally, were arrested and sent to prison in Oregon for three years. The children were split up. Her older brother and sister were sent to foster families in Oregon, where they had lived the longest. Veronica and her younger brother remained with their grandmother, but they were not told where their parents were and did not know if they would ever see them again. Three years later, her father—whose visa had expired while he was in prison—was deported to Mexico by ICE, where he has remained. Veronica's mother was allowed to stay in this country and settled in Denver with the children.

Several aspects of these experiences were particularly upsetting to Veronica. One was the way her older siblings were treated.

> They were shackled on their way to foster care, to Oregon. And they were only 15 and 12 years old. So the fact that you're shackled—handcuffed and on your feet—and going through the airport, and you're seeing everybody just looking at you while you're hopping up and down, I think that was very humiliating. Even though the government did take care of it, it's still very painful for them.[14]

She thought that the difficulties her brother and sister faced subsequently resulted from that shaming plus receiving minimal attention in their foster homes.

Another problem was that because Veronica's grandmother could not work, their little household lived on charity for the three years after her parents' arrest.

---

[14] The American Civil Liberties Union helped the family bring suit against the correctional services for maltreatment of the children:
http://aclu-co.org/court-cases/lamas-v-correctional-connections-l-l-c.

Everything that we got, the food we got, the clothes we got, school supplies and everything like that, was all donations, from churches and different places. I think that was one of the hardest things, because I remember going to school, and then people —like having new clothes and stuff—and my little brother and I would be with donated clothes. We had to just deal with that. People would make fun of us, like "Oh, look at your clothes!" [She cried here.] I had no choice but to think, "You don't understand what it's like to have your parents taken away."

Veronica finished her account by saying that after her father was deported,

My mother decided to stay in the United States because she had the vision of giving her children a better life—a life filled with opportunities and the ability to escape from poverty. My mother occasionally cleaned houses and earned about $80 per house, but it was difficult for her to support a family of five. Her hands were sometimes full of blisters. "I want you to go to school so that you don't have to clean bathrooms like I do," she would say to me, crying as she read the eviction notices. Although we constantly received eviction notices, our electricity would be disconnected, and our water would get shut down, my mother always provided food for us. I learned to fight for survival and to hunger for success from my mother, a woman who invented names for egg sandwiches so we would not know that was the only food we had.

This book joins the first volume in the set in demonstrating why it is essential to include the experiences of Latinas/os when thinking about Boulder County's history in the twentieth century. It contributes also to analysis of the four interpretive questions that began in the previous volume. It has enriched our picture of Latinas' roles, showing how they functioned within their families and neighborhoods and what they contributed in the areas of food, medicine, and religion. We noted the centrality of senior women as health care providers within the household and neighborhood and as organizers of home-based worship, though those duties declined after the mid-century.

The most conspicuous feature of intra-family relationships was their adaptability. Many adults weathered the potential challenge to their authority posed by having sons and/or daughters who had been to school and were better prepared to negotiate successfully in the Anglo dominated world around them. Many fathers and husbands took in stride the schooling of girls and women, just as they came to accept female work outside the home and women's leadership roles.[15] Grandparents remained important to their younger relatives emotionally and as teachers even after the authority of Latina elders due to their medical knowledge and spiritual guidance had decreased. The sole evidence of inter-generational tension, a topic suggested in the first book, comes from some young people's unwillingness to remain as fully engaged with the Catholic Church as their parents or grandparents wished.[16] Excessive male dominance and misuse of family resources, the negative face of *machismo*, was described only in private conversations.

Some patterns seen among Latinas/os in Boulder County, on the northeast margin of the borderlands, differed from what has been described in more heavily Latino communities. The composition of neighborhoods here, where people generally lived in mixed though poor sub-communities alongside people of different ethnicities and national backgrounds, contrasts with the residential experiences of Latinas/os who were surrounded by others like themselves in southwestern towns closer to the border or in the *barrios* of major cities. Nor did young Mexican American women in Boulder County during the 1940s and 1950s define themselves as deliberately distinct from Anglos, through dress and social behavior, as they did in some big cities. But there are suggestions of at least a weak local network: Latinas/os here had some cultural and religious contacts with people in Denver and agricultural Fort Lupton, especially during the first half of the twentieth century, and they interacted occasionally with groups based in Denver during the period of Chicano activism.[17]

The ethnic identities visible among Latinas/os in this setting contained strong social, cultural, and religious components. Preparing and sharing traditional foods was an enduring part of what it meant to be Latino, even after many women were working outside the home; love of familiar music and dancing likewise continued. Catholicism was part of the individual and family identity of most Boulder County Latinas/os throughout the twentieth century, whether or not they were regular church-goers. The willingness of children to go to school, despite the discrimination they sometimes faced there, had an impact upon identity formation. Young people taught by Anglo teachers alongside mainly

---

[15] Vol. I, Chs. 3A and D, 5A, and 6C.

[16] Vol. I, Chs. 5C and 6A.

[17] For the latter, see Vol. I, Ch. 7.

Anglo classmates needed to define themselves in a way that validated success within the dominant society and culture, even as they maintained aspects of their Hispanic heritage.

The people from Spanish-speaking backgrounds described in these two volumes left some positive legacies to Latinas/os living in Boulder County today. Because the Latino community is now very diverse, containing newcomers from multiple countries and backgrounds, not all of its members are affected by these inherited patterns. But especially for descendants of families that arrived prior to around 1980, even if they are married to non-Latinos, many of the attitudes and traditions highlighted here remain influential. Key features are: working hard for the good of your family in whatever your occupation may be; strong families that provide affection and practical support when needed; acknowledgment of the key roles played by women; religious faith, though not necessarily active church participation; a belief that education is the best way to attain a better future; a willingness to stand up and confront racism and discrimination; and development of an identity that allows you to function effectively in an environment shaped by Anglo expectations while still feeling pride in your own heritage. Among the cultural patterns that many local Latinas/os preserve in the twenty-first century are affection for traditional foods, especially at holidays, and enjoyment of Mexican or Latin music and dancing. Some of these cultural features have now made their way into Boulder County's population as a whole, enriching the lives of people who have no Spanish-speaking ancestors at all.

The interns described in the Epilogue to this volume provide grounds for optimism. The attitudes of these young people, some of whom will certainly become leaders—their dedication to education, ambitious goals, and social commitment—suggest that Latinas/os will make even greater contributions in the future. The potential they offer to the U.S. counteracts in powerful terms the anti-immigrant rhetoric voiced by some Americans in the 2010s.

This study has also furnished troubling information about racism and discrimination, not only in the past but in the present as well. To tackle the disparities that hinder Latinas/os and other people of color today, we must identity and challenge embedded ethnic and racial inequalities.[18]

[18] This paragraph is influenced by "Race Matters." As we saw with respect to the G.I. Bill (Vol. I, Ch. 5B), even projects with generally positive goals can have differential impacts for people of color if those measures are linked to institutions or programs that contain discriminatory features.

We need to commit to a serious examination and possible modification of attitudes, policies, and programs within in our own communities and at a higher level. The admirable goal of creating equitable opportunities for everyone lies at the core of a democratic society.

Appendix 6.1

Grade Level of Latino-Surnamed School Children, Three Towns, 1925-1964

Includes only those children for whom a grade was listed, expressed as percentage of the total with listed grade.

| | 1925 | | 1935 | | Boulder | |
	Longmont#	Lafayette	Longmont	Lafayette	Public school	Catholic school##
Grade in school, boys	N = 8	N = 44	N = 65	N = 97	N = 16	N = 4
K-3	75%	57%	57%	35%	50%	75%
4-6	25%	43%	29%	37%	25%	25%
7-8			9%	20%	13%	
9-12			5%	8%	13%	
Grade in school, girls	N = 11	N = 48	N = 84	N = 110	N = 10	N = 5
K-3	64%	52%	60%	30%	70%	80%
4-6	17%	31%	26%	34%	20%	20%
7-8	9%	6%*	11%	20%		
9-12		10%*	4%	16%	10%	

| Grade in school | 1944 or 1945 | | | 1955 | | | 1964 |
	Longmont	Boulder Public school	Boulder Catholic school##	Longmont	Boulder Public school	Boulder Catholic school##	Longmont
Grade in school, boys	N = 111	N = 24	N = 16	N = 110	N = 54	N = 3	N = 234
K-3	37%	21%	44%	38%	31%	33%	40%
4-6	31%	13%	38%	24%	26%	67%	27%
7-8	21%	8%	13%	13%	15%		15%
9-12	12%	58%	6%	25%	28% ~		19%
Grade in school, girls	N = 106	N = 27	N = 24	N = 141	N = 43	N = 11	N = 224
K-3	28%	19%	29%	36%	21%	27%	34%
4-6	34%	19%	33%	29%	25%	45%	29%
7-8	20%	15%	21%	18%	12%		20%
9-12	18%	48%	17%	16%	42%	27%	17%

\# In Longmont in 1925, 8 children were said to attend the "Sisters" school (presumably St. John's School), but without indication of grade level. Later figures do not differentiate between the schools.

\#\# Boulder's Catholic school as listed in these books was Sacred Heart.

* All of these lived in Lafayette town, not the rural district

~ Includes 1 at the university by end of the year

<u>Sources</u>: For Longmont: "Latino-surnamed children in Longmont schools" for 1905-1935; later information from Census books, LM, St. Vrain Valley School District Records. For Lafayette and Boulder, "Latino-surnamed children in Lafayette schools," 1915, 1925, 1935, 1944, and "Latino-surnamed children in Boulder schools," 1935, 1944, and 1955.

Appendix 6.2

Ages of Latino-Surnamed School Children, Three Towns, 1905-1964

Includes only those children whose age was listed, expressed as percentage of the total with listed age.

	1905	1915		1925	
	Longmont	Longmont	Lafayette	Longmont	Lafayette
Age of boys	N = 2	N = 4	N = 27	N = 25	N = 50
5-9		75%	44%	28%	22%
10-12	50%	25%	33%	32%	35%
13-15	50%		15%	20%	18%
16-18			7%	20%	16%
19-21					8%
Age of girls	N = 8	N = 8	N = 30	N = 27	N = 53
5-9	38%	25%	47%	30%	22%
10-12	25%	13%	20%	19%	20%
13-15	38%	25%	17%	19%	35%
16-18		25%	17%	4%	14%
19-21		13%		30% ~	10% ~

	1935			1944 or 1945		1955		1964
	Longmont	Lafayette	Boulder	Longmont	Boulder	Longmont	Boulder	Longmont
Age of boys	N = 71	N = 98	N = 25	N = 111	N = 48	N = 118	N = 56	N = 282
5-9	35%	22%	36%	33%	37%	34%	3%	35%
10-12	15%	28%	24%	20%	13%	19%	19%	23%
13-15	15%	18%	16%	21%	13%	15%	21%	19%
16-18	17%	12%	16%	18%	23%	23%	14%	12%
19-21	17%	19% #	8%	9%	13%	9%	42% ##	
Age of girls	N = 91	N = 115	N = 20	N = 117	N = 56	N = 148	N = 55	N = 268
5-9	25%	21% #	30%	23%	24%	33%	4%	29%
10-12	35%	27%	45%	17%	25%	25%	9%	26%
13-15	20%	22%	15%	22%	13%	20%	32%	22%
16-18	9%	17%	10%	24%	24%	14%	21%	16%*
19-21	11%	12%		14%	15%	8%	34%**	8% *

~ 5 of these 8 young women were already married

~~ Includes 1 woman aged 23

\# Includes 2 men aged 23 and 26

\#\# Includes 4 men aged 22, and 1 man aged 24

* 11 of the 64 girls/young women aged 16 to 21 were married

** Includes 3 women aged 22, 1 aged 23, and 1 aged 24

<u>Sources:</u> See App. 6.1.

List of Illustrations, with Credits

All images listed below that have a reference number beginning with "BCLHP" are available online at the Boulder County Latino History website:

http://bocolatinohistory.colorado.edu/

Go to the Search page and type the BCLHP reference into the box labelled "Search by ID."

Sources

Explanations

BCLHP Collection, Carnegie Library. Materials collected by the Boulder County Latino History Project, 2013-2014. Deposited at Carnegie Branch Library for Local History, Boulder Public Library.

BCLHP references.[1] These provide the ID number for items accessible on the Boulder County Latino History website, bocolatinohistory.colorado. edu. Go to the Search page and type the BCLHP reference into the box labelled "Search by ID." In the online version of this book, all references are hyperlinked directly to the original source.

If a given item contains multiple pages on the website, only the initial ID number is shown here; the following pages are linked to that one.

Carnegie Library. Carnegie Branch Library for Local History, Boulder Public Library

LM. Longmont Museum

LPL. Lafayette Public Library

MROHP. Maria Rogers Oral History Program, Carnegie Branch Library for Local History, Boulder Public Library

Information cited as from a conversation with Marjorie McIntosh on a stated date has been confirmed in writing and approved for use in this book by the authors of those statements.

All websites listed below were last accessed November 10-18, 2015.

[1] For entries with a BCLHP reference:
-- Items labelled as FP are family photographs loaned by community members and digitized by the BCLHP. The photographers are unknown unless specified.
-- Items labelled as LHS are photos loaned to the Longmont Hispanic Study in 1987-8 by a relative or descendent of the people shown. They were converted into slides by Oli Olivas Duncan for use in public presentations associated with the 1988 publication of *We, Too, Came to Stay: A History of the Longmont Hispanic Community*, which she edited. In 2014, the BCLHP was given permission to make digital copies of the slides, many of which showed unidentified people. The dates, locations, and photographers of these photos are unknown unless specified.

A. Sources about Boulder County Latinas/os

Abila, Mr. and Mrs. George. Oral history interview; Jessie Velez Lehmann, interviewer, 1978. Audio and transcript, MROHP. http://oralhistory.boulderlibrary.org/interview/oh0084.

Abila, Tom. Oral history interview; Jessie Velez Lehmann, interviewer, 1978. Audio and transcript, MROHP. http://oralhistory.boulderlibrary.org/interview/oh0085.

Alvarez, Teresa. Oral history interview; Theresa Banfield and Regina Vigil, interviewers, 1976. Audio and transcript, MROHP. http://oralhistory.boulderlibrary.org/interview/oh0137.

Alvarez, Teresa. Oral history interview; Theresa Banfield and Regina Vigil, interviewers, 1977. Audio and transcript, MROHP. http://oralhistory.boulderlibrary.org/interview/oh0086.

"Angie and Ray Perez at christening of their baby." BCLHP-LHS-386.

"Angie Perez bathing baby." BCLHP-LHS-043.

"Archuleta family history." Prepared for Boulder Hispanic Families project, 2012. Becky Archuleta, personal copy. BCLHP-FP-232.

"Archuleta siblings" in Boulder, 1954. Becky Archuleta, personal copy. BCLHP-FP-224.

"Archuleta, Ted. Eulogy" by his brother Jerry, 2009. BCLHP Collection, Carnegie Library. BCLHP-MKM-380.

"Arguello, Alfredo and Donaciana, and family. Biography." BCLHP Collection, Carnegie Library. BCLHP-MKM-381.

Arredondo, Yolanda. Oral history interview; Lindsay Leonard, interviewer, 2003. Audio and transcript, MROHP. http://oralhistory.boulderlibrary.org/interview/oh1218.

Arroyo (Arrollo), Candace. Oral history interview; Regina Vigil, interviewer, 1977. Audio and transcript, MROHP. http://oralhistory.boulderlibrary.org/interview/oh0087.

"Arroyo children, 1942." Clint Otis Dunn, photographer. Linda Arroyo-Holmstrom, personal copy. BCLHP-FP-123 (photo); BCLHP-FP-124 (text).

"Arroyo family at Chautauqua Park, 1947 (text)." Clint Otis Dunn, photographer. Linda Arroyo-Holmstrom, personal copy. BCLHP-FP-122 (description that accompanies Illus. 4.1).

Arroyo, Patrick. Oral history interview; Robin Branstator, interviewer, 1989. Audio and summary, MROHP. http://oralhistory.boulderlibrary.org/interview/oh0426.

Arroyo-Holmstrom, Linda. Oral history interview; Euvaldo Valdez, interviewer, 2013. Video and transcript, MROHP.
http://oralhistory.boulderlibrary.org/interview/oh1873.

"Asusena 'Susie' Espinoza," 1959. Gilbert Espinoza, personal copy. BCLHP-FP-091.

"Aztec dancers" in Longmont, 1980s. BCLHP-LHS-625.

"Becky Archuleta's First Communion remembrance," 1944. Becky Archuleta, personal copy. BCLHP-FP-229.

"Becky Ortega and friends" on Water Street, Boulder, 1947. Becky Archuleta, personal copy. BCLHP-FP-226.

"Bernal, E. E. and Eva. Biography," with photo, written by Phil Hernandez in 2012. Tom Martinez, personal copy. BCLHP-FP-045.

Bernal, Mr. and Mrs. Emerenciano. Oral history interview; Jessie Velez Lehmann, interviewer, 1977. Audio and transcript, MROHP.
http://oralhistory.boulderlibrary.org/interview/oh0081.

"Biographical sketch, Emma Gomez Martinez," written in 2012. Phil Hernandez, personal copy. BCLHP-MKM-455.

Blazón, Esther. Oral history interview; Linda Arroyo-Holmstrom, interviewer, 2013. Video and transcript, MROHP.
http://oralhistory.boulderlibrary.org/interview/oh1879.

Blazón, William ("Hank"). Oral history interview; Jaime Rios, interviewer, 2013. Video and transcript, MROHP.
http://oralhistory.boulderlibrary.org/interview/oh1877.

"Borrego, Albert, and Elvinia ("Bea") Martinez Borrego. Biography." BCLHP Collection, Carnegie Library. BCLHP-MKM-382.

"Boulder, film of places of historical importance" to Latinos, made in 2013. Linda Arroyo-Holmstrom and Phil Hernandez, narrators; Ana Gonzalez Dorta, videographer and editor. Produced for BCLHP. BCLHP-MKM-100.

"Boulder Latino families," 1910s-1950s. Compiled by Boulder Hispanic Families Project, 2012. BCLHP Collection, Carnegie Library. BCLHP-MKM-045.

"Boulder Public Library and Sacred Heart of Jesus Catholic Church," 1932. Becky Archuleta, personal copy. BCLHP-FP-234.

"Boulder's Chicano Community, 1979 film." Carnegie Branch Library for Local History, Boulder, DVD 978.863. BCLHP-MKM-047.

"Boulder's early black and Latino neighborhood," *Boulder Daily Camera*, Feb. 12, 2012. Phil Hernandez, personal copy. BCLHP-FP-005.

"Brenda Romero at her First Communion." BCLHP-LHS-136.

Cardenas, Alfonso. Oral history interview; Dorothy D. Ciarlo, interviewer, 2004. Video and summary, MROHP.
http://oralhistory.boulderlibrary.org/interview/oh1212.

Cardenas, Lou. Oral history interview; Oli Duncan, interviewer, c. 1987. In Duncan, ed., *We, Too, Came to Stay*, pp. 13-22. BCLHP-MKM-689.

"Casa Medina's softball team," 1987-8. BCLHP-LHS-051.

Casas Ibarra, Ana Karina. Oral history interview; Veronica Lamas, interviewer, 2013. Video and transcript, MROHP. http://oralhistory.boulderlibrary.org/interview/oh1870.

"Casey Middle School, 1943, and Boulder High School, 1937." Becky Archuleta, personal copy. BCLHP-FP-237.

"Casias, Angelina and Raymond. Biography," in *Lafayette, Colorado*, F74. BCLHP-SCW-186.

Chacon, Susie. Oral history interview; Regina Vigil, interviewer, 1977. Audio and transcript, MROHP. http://oralhistory.boulderlibrary.org/interview/oh0087.

"Chavez family home in Boulder, 1954." Mary Ellen Chavez, personal copy. BCLHP-FP-104.

"Children swimming in Longmont." BCLHP-LHS-053.

"Cholos y Cholas: youths' dress," *Longmont Times-Call*, May 9, 1987. BCLHP-MKM-243.

Cordero, Olga Melendez. Interview; Oli Duncan, interviewer, 2009. Rough draft transcript. BCLHP Collection, Carnegie Library. BCLHP-MKM-385.

Cordova, Patsy. Oral history interview; Oli Duncan, interviewer, c. 1987. In Duncan, ed., *We, Too, Came to Stay*, pp. 23-25. BCLHP-MKM-696.

"Cortez, Jose Hilario ("J. H."), and Maria Sabina Maes Cortez. Draft biography." BCLHP Collection, Carnegie Library. BCLHP-MKM-383.

"Created photo, Tony Montour, Sr.," with his mother, Emma, who died at his birth. Eleanor Montour, personal copy. BCLHP-FP-174.

"Dancing at a party." BCLHP-LHS-107.

"Daniel and Santos Suazo," Longmont, 1920-1930. LM, 2007.024.005. http://longmont.pastperfectonline.com/photo/23205A65-1750-4456-8182-324704926220.

De Luna, Deisy. Oral history interview; Veronica Lamas, interviewer, 2013. Video and transcript, MROHP. http://oralhistory.boulderlibrary.org/interview/oh1871.

"Dedication of Native and Hispanic Heritage Walk," 1999. Sharon Stetson, personal copy. BCLHP-FP-205.

"Delia and Edward Tafoya, Renewal of vows," 1977. Mable Stewart, personal copy. BCLHP-FP-135.

"Delia and Edward Tafoya's 50th wedding anniversary," 1977. Mable Stewart, personal copy. BCLHP-FP-134.

"Dixie Lee Aragon, honor award," *Boulder Daily Camera*, May 13, 1965. Dixie Lee Aragon, personal copy. BCLHP-FP-148.

"Dixie Lee Aragon receives Gambill Scholarship." *Boulder Daily Camera*, 1965. Dixie Lee Aragon, personal copy. BCLHP-FP-149.

Duncan, Oli Olivas. "Dad." Typescript, BCLHP Collection, Carnegie Library. Not online.

Duncan, Oli Olivas, ed. *We, Too, Came to Stay: A History of the Longmont Hispanic Community*. Privately published for the Longmont Hispanic Study, Longmont, [1988]. Individual interviews are available online, listed here under the person's name. BCLHP-MKM-689 through 711.

"Eddie Quintana's First Communion." BCLHP-LHS-048.

"Edward John Tafoya and Delia Mary Vargas, wedding commemoration," 1927. Mable Stewart, personal copy. BCLHP-FP-126.

El Aguila: The Eagle (written and illustrated by migrant teens), IDEAS, Nederland, CO, 1979. Individual interviews are available online, listed here under the person's name. Margaret Alfonso, personal copy. BCLHP Collection, Carnegie Library. BCLHP-MKM-612 through 654.

"Estrada, Cleo(patra). Autobiographical information." Typescript, BCLHP Collection, Carnegie Library. BCLHP-MKM-600.

"Farm family and Secundino Herrera in front of house." BCLHP-LHS-106.

"Father Wearing Hat with Four Children." BCLHP-LHS-433.

"First Communion, Josephine and Esther Arroyo," 1934. Linda Arroyo-Holmstrom, personal copy. BCLHP-FP-119 (photo); BCLHP-FP-120 (text).

"Five generations of women" in the Razo/Montour family. (Left to right, Alice Manzanares Blazon, b. 1963, Carmen Ramirez Razo, 1908-1985, Alice Razo Sanchez, 1926-1985, Eleanor Juarez Montour, 1944, Holly Lomme, 1980.) Eleanor Montour, personal copy. BCLHP-FP-185.

"Four Suazo sisters as young women." BCLHP-LHS-353.

Gallegos, Reina. Oral history interview; Oli Duncan, interviewer, c. 1987. In Duncan, ed., *We, Too, Came to Stay*, pp. 27-29. BCLHP-MKM-698.

"George Aragon with sons" Gilbert, Jerry, and Terry, 1945. Dixie Lee Aragon, personal copy. BCLHP-FP-150.

"Gilbert and Margie Espinoza at Central Park," Boulder, 1959. Gilbert Espinoza, personal copy. BCLHP-FP-086.

"Gilbert Espinoza in Viet Nam," 1969. Gilbert Espinoza, personal copy. BCLHP-FP-084.

"Gilbert Espinoza, State Champion, Wrestling Meet," 1965. Gilbert Espinoza, personal copy. BCLHP-FP-081.

"Gilbert Espinoza, State Wrestling Champion," 1964. Gilbert Espinoza, personal copy. BCLHP-FP-082.

"Gilbert Espinoza, wrestler at University of Colorado." Gilbert Espinoza, personal copy. BCLHP-FP-083.

"Gilbert Espinoza's military service," 1969. Gilbert Espinoza, personal copy. BCLHP-FP-085.

Gomez, Tony. Interview; Oli Duncan, interviewer, 2009. Draft transcript. BCLHP Collection, Carnegie Library. BCLHP-MKM-384.

Gonzales, Alex. Oral history interview; Oli Duncan, interviewer, c. 1987. In Duncan, ed., *We, Too, Came to Stay*, pp. 31-34. BCLHP-MKM-700.

Gonzales, Doris. Oral history interview; Jeff Dodge, interviewer, 2013. Audio and summary, MROHP.
http://oralhistory.boulderlibrary.org/interview/oh1920.

"Gonzales family portrait," 1934. Gonzales family, personal copy. BCLHP-FP-215.

Gonzalez Dorta, Ana. Oral history interview; Veronica Lamas, interviewer, 2013. Video and transcript, MROHP.
http://oralhistory.boulderlibrary.org/interview/oh1866.

"Graduates of Boulder Prep (High) School," *Boulder Daily Camera*, Sept. 9, 1935. BCLHP-SCW-046.

"Hank Blazón showing his family's religious objects," 2013. Jaime Rios, photographer, at interview with Blazón. BCLHP-FP-061.

Herrera, Secundino. Interview; Maura Diaz, Rosa Garcia, Lorenzo Huerta, Hilda Nunez, and Nati Santana, interviewers, 1979. In *El Aguila*, pp. 39-41. BCLHP-MKM-652.

Herrera, Secundino. Oral history interview; Oli Duncan, interviewer, c. 1987. In Duncan, ed., *We, Too, Came to Stay*, pp. 35-38. BCLHP-MKM-703.

"House at 1718 Water Street, Boulder," purchased by Juan and Clofes Archuleta in 1945. Becky Archuleta, personal copy. BCLHP-FP-225.

"Houses in camp, Industrial Mine." Louisville, 1905. LPL, LP03680.
http://www.cityoflafayette.com/PhotoViewScreen.aspx?PID=384.

"Intern questionnaires," Boulder County Latino History Project, summer, 2014. Ana Gonzalez Dorta, Deisy de Luna, Veronica Lamas, Emmanuel Melgoza, and Jason Romero, Jr. BCLHP Collection, Carnegie Library. Not online.

Jaramillo, Gregory. Oral history interview; Philip Hernandez, interviewer, 2013. Video and transcript, MROHP.
http://oralhistory.boulderlibrary.org/interview/oh1861.

"Jennie Razo (Romero) and Alicia Juarez (Sanchez)," 1941. Eleanor Montour, personal copy. BCLHP-FP-182.

"John S. Chavez Jr. and Knights of Columbus." Mary Ellen Chavez, personal copy. BCLHP-FP-113.

"Joseph and Sabina Cortez, 60th wedding anniversary," 1956. Hank Blazón, personal copy. BCLHP-FP-064.

"Juan Francisco Archuleta with guitar," 1942, at 2118 Goss Street, Boulder. Tom Martinez, personal copy. BCLHP-MKM-779.

Lafayette, Colorado: Treeless Plain to Thriving City. Centennial History, 1889-1989 (ed. James D. Hutchison). Lafayette, CO: Lafayette Historical Society, 1990. Articles about Latino families and events are available online, listed here under the person's name or event's title. BCLHP-SCW-162 through 218.

"Lafayette, film of places of historical importance" to Latinos, made in 2013. Eleanor Montour, narrator; Ana Gonzalez Dorta, videographer and editor. Produced for BCLHP. BCLHP-MKM-102.

"Lafayette's historic walking trail," 1996. Sharon Stetson, personal copy. BCLHP-FP-203.

Lamas, Veronica. Oral history interview; Deisy de Luna, interviewer, 2013. Video and transcript, MROHP. http://oralhistory.boulderlibrary.org/interview/oh1892.

"Latino graduates from Boulder High School," 1935-1980. Compiled by Boulder Hispanic Families Project, 2012. BCLHP Collection, Carnegie Library. Not online.

"Latino reunion," p. 1, *Boulder Daily Camera*, Aug. 7, 2003. BCLHP-MKM-774.

"Latino student graduates High School, 1956," *Lafayette Leader*, June 14, 1956. BCLHP-SCW-126.

"Latino student graduates High School, 1962," *Lafayette Leader*, June 18, 1962. BCLHP-SCW-127.

"Latino students graduate High School, 1964," Pts. 1 and 2, *Lafayette Leader*, June 18, 1964. BCLHP-SCW-128 and 129.

"Latino-surnamed children in Boulder schools": names and other information. Compiled by BCLHP from annual School Census Books, Boulder Valley School District, Education Center.
1935, BCLHP-Sch-001
1944, BCLHP-Sch-002
1955, BCLHP-Sch-003

"Latino-surnamed children in Lafayette schools": names and other information. Compiled by BCLHP from annual School Census Books, Boulder Valley School District, Education Center.
1915, BCLHP-Sch-004
1925, BCLHP-Sch-005
1935, BCLHP-Sch-006

"Latino-surnamed children in Longmont schools": names and other information. Compiled by BCLHP from annual School Census Books, LM, St. Vrain Valley School District Records.
1905, BCLHP-Sch-007
1915, BCLHP-Sch-008
1925, BCLHP-Sch-009
1935, BCLHP-Sch-010

"Latino youth enters Boulder Sanitarium," *Lafayette Leader*, Aug. 13, 1951. BCLHP-SCW-123.

Lehmann, Jessie Velez. Oral history interview; Regina Vigil, interviewer, 1978. Audio and transcript, MROHP.
http://oralhistory.boulderlibrary.org/interview/oh0089.

"Lincoln Elementary School, Boulder, Class Pictures." Janet Romero Perez, personal copies.
1956, BCLHP-FP-075
1957, BCLHP-FP-076
1958, BCLHP-FP-077
1959, BCLHP-FP-078

"Lincoln Elementary School, Boulder, Grades 3-4," 1954-1955. Janet Romero Perez, personal copy. BCLHP-FP-073.

"The Little Rose" [Sister Rosa Suazo], *The Voice of St. John the Baptist Catholic Church*, vol. 3, no. 6, Nov./Dec., 1996. Sister Rosa Suazo, personal copy. BCLHP-FP-016.

"Longmont, film of places of historical importance" to Latinos, made in 2013. Esther Blazón, narrator; Ana Gonzalez Dorta, videographer and editor. Produced for BCLHP. BCLHP-MKM-101.

"Los Inmigrantes," film showing interviews with Boulder Chicanos, 1979. Produced by Boulder's Chicano Community Project. Margaret Alfonso, personal copy. BCLHP-MKM-046.

Lucero, Elvira (artificial name). Oral history interview; Veronica Lamas, interviewer, 2013. Video and transcript, MROHP. BCLHP-MKM-121.

"Madrigal family of Boulder. Biographies." Boulder Hispanic Families Project, 2012. BCLHP Collection, Carnegie Library. BCLHP-MKM-404.

"Maestas, Pedro (Roy), Ruby, and Abe. Biography." Boulder Hispanic Families Project, 2012. BCLHP Collection, Carnegie Library. BCLHP-MKM-370.

Maestas, Roy. Oral history interview; Jessie Velez Lehmann, interviewer, 1978. Audio and summary, MROHP.
http://oralhistory.boulderlibrary.org/interview/oh0082.

Maestas, Virginia. Oral history interview; Regina Vigil, interviewer, 1978. Audio and transcript, MROHP.
http://oralhistory.boulderlibrary.org/interview/oh0083.

Maestas, Virginia. Oral history interview; Jeff Dodge, interviewer, 2013. Audio and summary, MROHP. http://oralhistory.boulderlibrary.org/interview/oh1923.

"Man playing guitar and woman playing accordion. BCLHP-LHS-634.

"Man with large fish." BCLHP-LHS-610.

"Map of Boulder's Water + Goss Streets neighborhood by ethnicity, 1955." Prepared by Phil Hernandez, 2012. Phil Hernandez, personal copy. BCLHP-MKM-401.

"Map of central Boulder by ethnicity, 1955." Prepared by Phil Hernandez, 2012. Phil Hernandez, personal copy. BCLHP-MKM-400.

"Map of Lafayette in 1906?" LPL, Map Storage. BCLHP-SCW-149.

"Map of Lafayette in 1918." LPL, Map Storage. BCLHP-SCW-144.

"Martinez, Canuto and Gregoria. Biography," written by Phil Hernandez in 2012. Tom Martinez, personal copy. BCLHP-FP-044.

"Martinez, Emma Gomez. Letter to Her Children." Tom Martinez, personal copy. BCLHP Collection, Carnegie Library. BCLHP-MKM-446.

Martinez, Emma Gomez. Oral history interview; Euvaldo Valdez, interviewer, 2013. Video and transcript, MROHP. http://oralhistory.boulderlibrary.org/interview/oh1893.

"Martinez, Fabricio, and Letia Madrid on wedding day," Longmont, 1947. LM, 1995.012.003. http://longmont.pastperfectonline.com/photo/E0E7A57A-53F3-403D-8429-217918741939.

"Martinez, Juan and Josephine; Marcella Martinez Diaz. Biography." Boulder Hispanic Families Project, 2012. BCLHP Collection, Carnegie Library. BCLHP-MKM-371.

Martinez, Mary. Oral history interview; interviewer unknown, 1988. Video and detailed summary, MROHP. http://oralhistory.boulderlibrary.org/interview/oh1912.

Martinez, Sally, and other Pioneer Families. Oral history interview; Anne Dyni, interviewer, 1990. Audio and summary, MROHP. http://oralhistory.boulderlibrary.org/interview/oh0530.

Medina, Maria. Oral history interview; interviewer unknown, c. 1978. Audio and summary, MROHP. http://oralhistory.boulderlibrary.org/interview/oh0080.

Medina, Miguel. Oral history interview; Jaime Rios, interviewer, 2013. Video and transcript, MROHP. http://oralhistory.boulderlibrary.org/interview/oh1878.

Melgoza, Emmanuel. Oral history interview; Veronica Lamas, interviewer,

2013. Video and transcript, MROHP.
http://oralhistory.boulderlibrary.org/interview/oh1863.

"Mexicans celebrate Independence Day," *Longmont Ledger*, Sept. 20, 1935.
BCLHP-MKM-190.

"Migrant Health Clinic gives guidance, care," *Longmont Times-Call*, July 20,
1977. BCLHP-MKM-206.

Montour, Eleanor. Oral history interview; Euvaldo Valdez, interviewer, 2013.
Video and transcript, MROHP.
http://oralhistory.boulderlibrary.org/interview/oh1860.

Moreno, Heriberto ("Beto"). Oral history interview; Ray Rodriguez,
interviewer, 2013. Video and transcript, MROHP.
http://oralhistory.boulderlibrary.org/interview/oh1897.

Moreno, Marta Valenzuela. Oral history interview; Linda Arroyo-Holmstrom,
interviewer, 2013. Video and transcript, MROHP.
http://oralhistory.boulderlibrary.org/interview/oh1881.

"Mr. and Mrs. Alex Gonzales' 50th wedding anniversary," 1974. Gonzales
family, personal copy. BCLHP-FP-214.

"Occupations and Employers of Latino-Surnamed Adults, Three Towns."
Compiled by BCLHP from *Polk's City Directories*.
1936, BCLHP-Occ-002
1946, BCLHP-Occ-003
1955, BCLHP-Occ-004
1965, BCLHP-Occ-005
1975, BCLHP-Occ-006

"Olivas, Ralph and Rose. Biographical account," by their daughter, Oli Olivas
Duncan, c. 1987. In Duncan, ed., *We, Too, Came to Stay*, pp. 39-44. BCLHP-
MKM-706.

"Ortega, John, family of. Biography," in *Lafayette, Colorado*, F332.
BCLHP-SCW-201.

Ortega, Roseann Chavez. Oral history interview; Anne Dyni, interviewer, 1986.
Audio and transcript, MROHP.
http://oralhistory.boulderlibrary.org/interview/oh0579.

"Parents wave goodbye to children on first day of school," *Boulder Daily
Camera*, Sept. 5, 1958. BCLHP-SCW-048.

"People dancing at a party." BCLHP-LHS-484.

Perez, Arthur. Oral history interview; Jaime Rios, interviewer, 2013. Video and
transcript, MROHP.
http://oralhistory.boulderlibrary.org/interview/oh1882.

"Pleasant View Ridge Elementary, Longmont, 1949, Grades 1-4." LM,
1995.015.004.

http://longmont.pastperfectonline.com/photo/8E3363DB-64A6-4147-8744-623435449927.

"Pleasant View Ridge Elementary, Longmont, 1949, Grades 5-8." LM, 1995.015.005. http://longmont.pastperfectonline.com/photo/4190D67D-3D4E-4419-967D-350378253500.

"Police chief attacked at Mexican celebration," *Longmont Times-Call*, May 6, 1937. BCLHP-MKM-208.

"Portrait of the Suazo children," Longmont, 1930-1940. LM, 2007.024.006. http://longmont.pastperfectonline.com/photo/54EAA898-43E7-4F1A-ADA9-118625271190.

"Racism in the school system," by Dixie Lee Aragon, 2012. Dixie Lee Aragon, personal copy. BCLHP-FP-147.

Ramirez, Carmen. Oral history interview; Linda Arroyo-Holmstrom, interviewer, 2013. Video and transcript, MROHP. http://oralhistory.boulderlibrary.org/interview/oh1880.

"Ray Perez with baby." BCLHP-LHS-056.

"Rhonda Gonzales' and another girl's First Communion." BCLHP-LHS-049.

Romero, Jason, Jr. Oral history interview; Veronica Lamas, interviewer, 2013. Video and transcript, MROHP. http://oralhistory.boulderlibrary.org/interview/oh1865.

"Rosales, Larry and Linda. Biography," in *Lafayette, Colorado*, F375. BCLHP-SCW-204.

Salazar, Edwina. Oral history interview; Euvaldo Valdez, interviewer, 2013. Video and transcript, MROHP. http://oralhistory.boulderlibrary.org/interview/oh1854.

"Salazar, Jose Benito and Isabelle (Rivera). Biography," in *Lafayette, Colorado*, F379. BCLHP-SCW-206.

"Sally Martinez as an Elderly Widow," *Boulder Daily Camera*, Feb. 10, 1991. Sharon Stetson, personal copy. BCLHP-FP-208.

Salomon, Margarita Macias. Interview; Oli Duncan, interviewer, 2009. Draft transcript. BCLHP Collection, Carnegie Library. BCLHP-MKM-386.

Sanchez, Dalia. Oral history interview; Veronica Lamas, interviewer, 2013. Video and transcript, MROHP. http://oralhistory.boulderlibrary.org/interview/oh1876.

"Sanctuary, St. John's Catholic Church," Longmont, early 20th c.? LM, 1971.034.049. http://longmont.pastperfectonline.com/photo/FE64531F-1718-4CE2-A380-640576409562.

"Saragosa, Pete (originally Pedro Zaragoza). Property records" from the Boulder County Assessor's Office, copied by Leslie Ogeda. BCLHP Collection, Carnegie Library. Not online.

Sarceno, Kelly. Oral history interview; Veronica Lamas, interviewer, 2013. Video and transcript, MROHP. http://oralhistory.boulderlibrary.org/interview/oh1868.

Serrano, Salvador. Oral history interview, Veronica Lamas, interviewer, 2013. Video and transcript, MROHP. http://oralhistory.boulderlibrary.org/interview/oh1864.

"Shirley Roybal at baptism" of her baby. BCLHP-LHS-129.

Silva, Dolores. Oral history interview; Margaret Alfonso, interviewer, 2013. Video and transcript, MROHP. http://oralhistory.boulderlibrary.org/interview/oh1886.

"Sister Maria Regina Rodriguez," daughter of Matias and Silvera Rodriguez, aged 87 in 2014. Eleanor Montour, personal copy. BCLHP-FP-181.

"Sister Rosa Suazo (center) in Senior Folklorico Dance Group, 2009." Sister Rosa Suazo, personal copy. BCLHP-FP-018.

"Sister Rosa Suazo (in white, on right)," St. Francis Convent, Milwaukee Wisc., 1955. Sister Rosa Suazo, personal copy. BCLHP-FP-017.

"Six children in front of car." BCLHP-LHS-191.

"St. John's Catholic church and parsonage," Longmont, early 20th c.? LM, 1971.034.048. http://longmont.pastperfectonline.com/photo/E403E019-7BDC-4B32-AB20-094546706444.

"Suazo family," including Daniel, Santos, and Sister Rosa, Longmont, 1950-60. LM, 2007.024.007. http://longmont.pastperfectonline.com/photo/5AB32EC8-A148-4A8B-B622-105342309007.

"Suazo family house," 1912 9th Avenue, Longmont, 1977. LM, 2007.024.004. http://longmont.pastperfectonline.com/photo/61943B70-61DF-4F42-9D58-803532647920.

"Suazo family in front of Lloyd Dicken's house," Longmont, 1940-1945. LM, 2007.024.002. http://longmont.pastperfectonline.com/photo/41416C0C-A719-4CEA-8E28-746656143237.

"Sugar Beet Baseball Leagues," *Colorado Country Life*, April, 2012. Phil Hernandez, personal copy. BCLHP-FP-040.

"Tafoya family Christmas," 1956. Mable Stewart, personal copy. BCLHP-FP-128.

Tafoya, Mary Gonzales. Interview; Oli Duncan, interviewer, 2009. Transcript. BCLHP Collection, Carnegie Library. BCLHP-MKM-387.

"Three boys in matching plaid jackets" in front of car. BCLHP-LHS-190.

"Three young children playing in yard." BCLHP-LHS-135.

"Tina Perez and other teens playing poker." BCLHP-LHS-169.

Toledo, David. Oral history interview; interviewer unknown, c. 1978. Audio and summary, MROHP. http://oralhistory.boulderlibrary.org/interview/oh0080.

"Tony Quintana holding baby." BCLHP-LHS-114.

"Tony Quintana with three sons." BCLHP-LHS-093.

"Two girls in an outhouse." BCLHP-LHS-176.

"Two men standing in front of a car." BCLHP-LHS-546.

"Two toddlers on the bumper of a car." BCLHP-LHS-193.

"Two young men and a young woman playing guitars." BCLHP-LHS-472.

Valdez, Emma Suazo. Oral history interview; Oli Duncan, interviewer, c. 1987. In Duncan, ed., *We, Too, Came to Stay*, pp. 49-50. BCLHP-MKM-710.

Vigil, Jennie, Angela Apodaca, and Shirley Trevino. Oral history interview; Anne Dyni, interviewer, 2001. Video and transcript, MROHP. http://oralhistory.boulderlibrary.org/interview/oh1022.

"Vigil, Rudy and Theresa. Biography," in *Lafayette, Colorado*, F431. BCLHP-SCW-208.

Villagran, Lucia and Lily. Oral history interview; Esther Blazón, interviewer, 2013. Video and transcript, MROHP. http://oralhistory.boulderlibrary.org/interview/oh1884.

"Walking tours to highlight Lafayette's historic buildings." Sharon Stetson, personal copy. BCLHP-FP-204.

"Wedding and 50th wedding anniversary of Tony Montour, Sr., and Julia Rodriguez Montour" (1940s and 1990s). Eleanor Montour, personal copy. BCLHP-FP-172.

"Wedding of Becky and Dave Ortega," Sacred Heart of Jesus Church, Boulder, 1953. Becky Archuleta, personal copy. BCLHP-FP-230.

"Wedding of Clofes Luisa Mondragon and Juan Francisco Archuleta," 1923. Becky Archuleta, personal copy. BCLHP-FP-223.

"Wedding of Emma Gomez and John Martinez," 1946. Thomas Martinez, personal copy. BCLHP-FP-140.

"Wedding of John Anthony Rivera and Marilyn Martinez Rivera," 1958. Sharon Stetson, personal copy. BCLHP-FP-195.

"Wedding of John S. and Tillie Chavez, 1940." Mary Ellen Chavez, personal copy. BCLHP-FP-102.

B. Other Books, Articles, and On-Line Materials

Abbott, Carl, Stephen J. Leonard, and Thomas J. Noel. *Colorado: A History of the Centennial State.* 5th edit., Boulder: University Press of Colorado, 2013.

Acuña, Rodolfo F. *Occupied America: A History of Chicanos.* 7th edit., Boston: Longman/Pearson, 2011.

Adelfang, Karen, ed. *Erie: Yesterday and Today.* Typed report, Erie, 1974. Copy at Carnegie Branch Library for Local History, Boulder Public Library.

Alamillo, José M. *Making Lemonade out of Lemons: Mexican American Labor and Leisure in a California Town, 1880-1960.* Urbana: University of Illinois Press, 2006.

Alvarez, Luis. *The Power of the Zoot: Youth Culture and Resistance during World War II.* Berkeley: University of California Press, 2008.

Boulder County TRENDS 2013: The Community Foundation's Report on Key Indicators. Boulder, CO: The Community Foundation, 2013.

Chavez, Rebecca D. "Making Them Count: A Baseline Study of the Latino Community in Longmont, Colorado, 1910 to 1940." M.A. thesis, New Mexico State University, 2014.

Donato, Rubén. *Mexicans and Hispanos in Colorado Schools and Communities, 1920-1960.* Albany: State University of New York Press, 2007.

Escobedo, Elizabeth R. *From Coveralls to Zoot Suits: The Lives of Mexican American Women on the World War II Home Front.* Chapel Hill: University of North Carolina Press, 2013.

Gonzales, Rodolfo (Corky). "I Am Joaquín." http://history.msu.edu/hst327/files/2009/05/I-Am-Joaquin.pdf

Hamilton, Candy. *Footprints in the Sugar: A History of the Great Western Sugar Company.* Ontario, OR: Hamilton Bates Publishers, 2009.

Hayes-Bautista, David E. *El Cinco de Mayo: An American Tradition.* Berkeley: University of California Press, 2012.

Lopez, Jody L., and Gabriel A. Lopez, with Peggy A. Ford. *White Gold Laborers: The Spanish Colony of Greeley, Colorado.* Bloomington, IN: AuthorHouse, 2007.

McIntosh, Marjorie K. *Latinos of Boulder County, Colorado, 1900-1980,* Vol. I: *History and Contributions.* Palm Springs, CA: Old John Publishing, 2016.

Polk's City Directories for Boulder [and adjoining communities], 1904, 1916 (using *Polk's Boulder County Directory*), *1926, 1936, 1946, 1955, 1965,* and *1975; Polk's City Directories for Longmont, 1965* and *1975* (R. L. Polk & Co., place of publication not given).

"Race Matters." Power Point presentation produced by the Annie E. Casey Foundation, no date, to go with the Race Matters Toolkit. http://www.aecf.org/resources/race-matters-powerpoint-presentation

Ramirez, Catherine S. *The Woman in the Zoot Suit: Gender, Nationalism, and the Cultural Politics of Memory*. Durham, NC: Duke University Press, 2009.

Romero, Tom I. "Of Greater Value than the Gold of Our Mountains: The Right to Education in Colorado's Nineteenth-Century Constitution." *University of Colorado Law Review*, 83 (2012): 781-843.

Romero, Tom I. "No Brown Towns: Anti-Immigrant Ordinances and Equality of Educational Opportunity for Latina/os." *Journal of Gender, Race, and Justice*, 12:1 (2008): 13-56.

Rosales, F. Arturo. *¡Pobre Raza! Violence, Justice, and Mobilization among México Lindo Immigrants, 1900-1936*. Austin: University of Texas Press, 1999.

Taylor, Paul S. *Mexican Labor in the United States*. Vol. I, Berkeley: University of California Press, 1930.

They Came to Stay: Longmont, Colorado, 1858-1920. St. Vrain Valley Historical Association, Longmont, CO: Longmont Printing Company, 1971.

Index

CPSIA information can be obtained
at www.ICGtesting.com
Printed in the USA
LVOW04*2327260216

476930LV00003B/4/P